TEMPLES
ON THE
OTHER SIDE

OTHER BOOKS BY SYLVIA BROWNE

Adventures of a Psychic (with Antoinette May)
Contacting Your Spirit Guide (book-with-CD)
Conversations with the Other Side
Exploring the Levels of Creation
God, Creation, and Tools for Life (Book 1)
If You Could See What I See
Meditations
Mother God
The Nature of Good and Evil (Book 3)
Secrets & Mysteries of the World
Secret Societies . . . and How They Affect Our Lives Today
Soul's Perfection (Book 2)
Spiritual Connections
Sylvia Browne's Book of Angels
Sylvia Browne's Lessons for Life

All of the above are available at your
local bookstore, or may be ordered by visiting:

Hay House UK: **www.hayhouse.co.uk**
Hay House USA: **www.hayhouse.com**®
Hay House Australia: **www.hayhouse.com.au**
Hay House South Africa: **www.hayhouse.co.za**
Hay House India: **www.hayhouse.co.in**

TEMPLES
ON THE
OTHER SIDE

How Wisdom from 'Beyond the Veil'
Can Help You Right Now

SYLVIA BROWNE

HAY HOUSE

Australia • Canada • Hong Kong • India
South Africa • United Kingdom • United States

Published and distributed in the United Kingdom by:
Hay House UK Ltd, 292B Kensal Rd, London W10 5BE. Tel.: (44) 20 8962 1230;
Fax: (44) 20 8962 1239. www.hayhouse.co.uk

Published and distributed in the United States of America by:
Hay House, Inc., PO Box 5100, Carlsbad, CA 92018-5100. Tel.: (1) 760 431 7695
or (800) 654 5126; Fax: (1) 760 431 6948 or (800) 650 5115. www.hayhouse.com

Published and distributed in Australia by:
Hay House Australia Ltd, 18/36 Ralph St, Alexandria NSW 2015. Tel.: (61) 2 9669
4299; Fax: (61) 2 9669 4144. www.hayhouse.com.au

Published and distributed in the Republic of South Africa by:
Hay House SA (Pty), Ltd, PO Box 990, Witkoppen 2068. Tel./Fax: (27) 11 467
8904. www.hayhouse.co.za

Published and distributed in India by:
Hay House Publishers India, Muskaan Complex, Plot No.3, B-2, Vasant Kunj,
New Delhi – 110 070. Tel.: (91) 11 4176 1620; Fax: (91) 11 4176 1630.
www.hayhouse.co.in

Distributed in Canada by:
Raincoast, 9050 Shaughnessy St, Vancouver, BC V6P 6E5. Tel.: (1) 604 323 7100;
Fax: (1) 604 323 2600

© Sylvia Browne, 2008

The moral rights of the author have been asserted.

The author of this book does not dispense medical advice or prescribe the use of
any technique as a form of treatment for physical or medical problems without
the advice of a physician, either directly or indirectly. The intent of the author is
only to offer information of a general nature to help you in your quest for
emotional and spiritual wellbeing. In the event you use any of the information
in this book for yourself, which is your constitutional right, the author and the
publisher assume no responsibility for your actions.

A catalogue record for this book is available from the British Library.

ISBN 978-1-4019-1556-8

Printed and bound in Great Britain by TJ International, Padstow, Cornwall.

To my son Chris Dufresne,
who helps me keep
everything running

CONTENTS

PART III: HALLS THAT CAN TRULY HELP US ON EARTH

PART IV: MEDITATIONS FOR VISITING THE TEMPLES

PREFACE

In some of my previous books, I wrote extensively about what I call "the Other Side," including particulars about our journey to it, as well as what it's like over there. But I recently realized that it was time for a great deal of this information to be updated—especially that which concerned the many temples or halls that provide so much help and comfort. (I use the terms *hall* and *temple* interchangeably because they're used synonymously on the Other Side.) Well, my spirit guide Francine has always told me that in order for a question to be answered, first it has to be asked, so that's just what I did.

For those of you who don't know about Francine, she's been with me my entire life even though I first "heard" her when I was seven years old. You see, I'm *clairaudient,* which means that I hear my spirit guide talk to me. However, I can't bear to listen to her directly for very long because her voice comes into my right ear and sounds like a more annoying version of Alvin and the Chipmunks. Nevertheless, I *did* ask her about other temples or buildings of importance, and I was shocked when she told me about numerous sites that I'd never heard of before!

I thought that there were only four or five significant halls on the Other Side, but Francine said, "Oh no, there are at least 20, each with a different purpose." And when I wondered why she hadn't told me about them before, Miss Smarty said, "You never asked." (I think that in the future, I'll just automatically tack on to my questions: "Is that all, or is there more information that you aren't telling me?")

Then as I began to compile further research, it occurred to me that I'd never written about the temples on the Other Side at length. Yes, I'd previously skimmed over the few that I knew about, but I hadn't gone into detail about their functions. So I decided to bite the bullet, admit that I hadn't asked enough questions, and author another book to update previous information and get this mass of new data out there.

Why now? As I've said before on *The Montel Williams Show,* belief in the afterlife is becoming so strong that the veil from the Earth plane to the Other Side is thinning rapidly. Notice what's been happening in the last ten years or so, from increased interest in my own appearances and books to all sorts of people coming out of the proverbial closet and inquiring about passed-over loved ones, ghosts, spirits, hauntings, and the like. Just look at TV shows such as *Medium, Ghost Whisperer,* and even *Joan of Arcadia,* which was about a young woman talking to God—these never would have been possible 10 or 15 years ago because most of society wasn't brave enough to look into things that were outside of the mainstream.

As men and women become more educated, they tend to ask more questions. I'm the first to admit that many of my readers and fans have led the charge, and their queries have spurred on my own search for answers. The result is that we now have new and more extensive information about our journey back Home to the Other Side (when we cross over), specifically regarding what goes on in those beautiful temples. Getting into the deeper meanings of these buildings is not only fascinating but also spiritually enlightening, because it proves that there *is* order everywhere in God's universe.

What you're about to read in these pages may seem far-fetched at first, but I can almost guarantee that when you get into it, its logic will entice you, amaze you, and make you a more avid believer.

INTRODUCTION

Before I go any further, I'd like to explain how the idea for this book first came about. You see, from time to time I conduct salons at my office in Campbell, California, in which a group of people spend the day with me speaking about spirituality. Occasionally I'll go into trance, and my spirit guide Francine will enter my body to talk about different things and answer questions from the attendees. It was at one of these salons a few months ago that Francine began to discuss certain edifices that could help both those of us on Earth *and* on the Other Side get through stress, grief, and other problems.

You may not know that part of my paranormal or psychic abilities involves my ability to go into trance; in fact, I'm one of the few true deep-trance mediums in the world at the moment. Such mediumship is so rare nowadays because most psychics instead prefer to channel messages and keep their consciousness within their bodies while doing so. A true trance medium gives up his or her body completely to another entity and has no memory of what transpires while that entity is residing there. It's really a lost art that saw its peak in the days of Spiritualism, which was popular in the late 19th and early 20th centuries.

Now some call deep-trance mediumship "unconscious chan-neling," while "conscious channeling" means that consciousness is retained. (*Channeling* is actually a relatively new term to the psychic world, having come out in the 1960s and '70s with the advent of New Age groups.) Leonore Piper, Arthur Ford, Eileen Garrett, and Edgar Cayce would be considered deep-trance medi-ums or unconscious channelers, while John Edward and James Van Praagh would be seen as conscious channelers.

Taking a slight detour, I'd like to talk about prophets for a moment. *Prophecy* comes from a Greek word that means "spokes-person for the gods." God has indeed touched special individuals in such a way throughout human history in order to provide us with some guidance without taking away the test of life on Earth. You see, God's grace, intelligence, and order is always at work. Even though certain events can seem like the worst tragedies, the deeper you delve into spiritual knowledge, the more you'll come to the realization that even these stressful events can open you up to life and help you grow. We're all born with wisdom and strength that we're often not even aware of until we're tested, and how can we learn what we're spiritually made of if we're never challenged?

If God just spoke to all of us en masse and gave us specific directions, we wouldn't be able to learn the Universe's ultimate truths through our own experiences. So He has sent us numerous messengers throughout history to try to get His words across . . . some have been listened to and some have not. Unfortunately, many charlatans and false psychics or prophets who claimed to be messengers have also surfaced over the years, serving only to bilk others for their own gain. It seems that where human evolution is concerned, you'll always find those who want to curtail it or take advantage of those who seek it.

As I've said many times, nothing can *ever* be done without God, yet it's a known fact that many so-called prophets have tended to align themselves with less-than-holy forces, whether it was to gain favor or money . . . or simply out of fear. Look at all the seers and astrologers Hitler used, to no avail. Of course, any psychic can often be wrong because God is the only source that's right all of the time, but anyone who's using his or her talents for power, money, vanity, greed, or the like is not a true prophet *or* psychic.

If someone were to ask me the best way to judge whether or not a medium is for real, I'd simply answer, "Show me how long of a waiting list he or she has." Good psychics won't have to advertise their services, as word of mouth will always get around. The more satisfied an individual's clients are, the more those clients will spread news of the medium's abilities to others.

Speaking for myself, I genuinely believe that I've been given my psychic abilities from God. To that end, I've dedicated my life to Him and to getting as much of my "Divine guidance" out to as many people as I can. I've also tried to back up this information with researched truths whenever possible. I feel that if I do not (and many psychics don't), then I'll never be able to validate that I *do* have the ability to "quantum leap" into the future or the past. I attempt to do the best I can in all phases of my abilities each and every time I use them. Am I ever wrong? Of course I am! I'm human and certainly not perfect. However, I wouldn't survive very long as a psychic if I wasn't right much more than I was wrong.

Certainly, I've made a lot of mistakes, which I've already written about honestly and thoroughly. Yet even with my divorces and personal and financial woes, life's problems have never impeded my love for God or my dedication to Him. He has always sustained me through good times and bad, and I will always try with all my heart and soul to take the information and guidance that He gives me to share with all of you.

Getting back to the salon with Francine, 40 or so people had come to ask her questions that day, and it seemed to some that she started the session with an apology. Actually, she was just explaining why she hadn't been able to come in more frequently and why she has to give out particularly pertinent information whenever she does.

We used to have open trances for the public, as well as private research sessions for our ministers, but these have had to be curtailed because of my many readings and lecture tours, as well as all the books I write. So my dear guide told this group, "Each time I come in trance, I must now do so with different facets of spiritual knowledge and information. I used to be able to do this in research trances with Sylvia's ministers, but because she's been so busy, I haven't had a chance to give out the ongoing theology."

Someone decided to take the opportunity to ask where we go for research or learning on the Other Side . . . and that set the whole explanation of all these temples into motion. Francine began to talk about the Hall of Wisdom, the Hall of Justice, and the Council of Elders (all of which will be thoroughly covered in this book) and how they could help someone resolve issues. We always tape Francine's words, and as I was listening to this particular session, I heard about buildings that I never knew existed and became utterly fascinated. I found it quite comforting to hear about these magnificent edifices that were created for our own specific needs, and became very excited about the fact that we can access them even when we are in life (that is, still here on Earth).

Since Francine had only mentioned a few new temples due to time constraints, I immediately asked her whether there were more that she hadn't covered. In a very casual manner, she replied, "Of course." Somewhat irked, I wondered why she hadn't come out with this information earlier. She just matter-of-factly responded, "You didn't ask."

Oh boy. It's sometimes very frustrating to realize that you have the ability to tap into a wealth of knowledge via a guide who can access almost any subject you can think of, only to be thwarted because you failed to ask a specific question. It's certainly not Francine's fault, for she's only reacting to my perceived wishes. She tries to do her best in volunteering information that she thinks I might be interested in from time to time, but she can't read my mind and certainly doesn't want to constantly babble in my ear like a talking encyclopedia on topics that I may not care about. It really *is* my fault for not asking the right questions, since she's never failed to answer anything that I've put forth to her.

One of the reasons why I formed research groups over the years is because I felt that many heads were better than one when asking Francine questions for clarification. The information that she's disseminated over the years has allowed me to publish my books, stabilize the philosophy of the Society of Novus Spiritus (my church), and conduct my spiritual teaching on a wide scale. Consequently, I spent this time to get further details from her about the temples on the Other Side, especially those that can help us on *this* side of the veil. As always, she's done her job very well.

After Death . . .

This would be a good time to familiarize you (or, if you're a long-term fan of mine, *re*familiarize you) with a few of the subjects I tend to return to over and over. Take, for example, what happens after we die.

Most of us will experience something very similar to the following: After passing from this life, we'll see a bright light at the end of what appears to be a tunnel of whirling light. (When I had my near-death experience, I actually saw this tunnel form and emanate from my solar-plexus region.) Since the majority of us have lived prior lives, we'll remember that this is the way to the Other Side and happily go through the tunnel toward the bright light.

The most profound effect that we'll feel during this time is one of peace and love . . . cares and worries will drop away almost like magic, and we'll sense a great uplifting of our souls and a feeling of weightlessness. We're finally going Home from a temporal existence on a very negative plane, and no longer will we suffer pain of any kind. Our loved ones on the Other Side soon join us for the most wondrous of reunions, and we enter into the true reality of God's ever-present and everlasting love. The joy we experience will exact an immediate healing on almost any trauma that the soul has suffered in our just-completed life.

Interestingly, only adults seem to go through the tunnel—young children who die tend to go over a sort of footbridge, where they're usually met by a remembered loved one or guide. Francine says that children need to have the footbridge to orient them from point A to point B because a tunnel might be too frightening and closed in for them.

A very few who have experienced severe trauma as part of a difficult death may have some disorientation and find it harder to go through the tunnel and into the light; in those cases, a passed-over loved one will usually try to guide them through. Fewer still won't go into the tunnel and toward the light at all due to confusion, perhaps believing that they're not actually dead. These rare instances account for what humankind calls "ghosts"—less than one percent of all people who die fall into this category.

Since we've made this trip several times before, it just makes sense that our memory immediately kicks in and everything is so familiar that we know exactly where we're going. It's like when I drive to Los Angeles from my home in San Jose, California, which I do maybe ten times a year: How could I ever forget where I'm going when I've done it so many times?

Also, after we die all parts of our spiritual memory are working. Francine says that we're lucky if we're using 20 percent of our brainpower while incarnated on Earth. Well, imagine *100* percent of our brains working—*all* the people, lives, places, and circumstances from our *total* experiencing existence floods back. Memories of past lives, our loved ones and friends, our pets, what we do on the Other Side . . . it all comes rushing back into full focus.

People worry that their family member dying with Alzheimer's won't remember anything upon returning Home, which is as ridiculous as thinking that someone who can't walk or who's lost a limb will be the same after death. No, as I've stated many times before, we all go back to 30 years of age and return to our full, glorified form when we get Home. The human body and brain we leave behind are only parts of the old "car" we walk away from when we die—and really never look back at in any regretful way.

The Other Side

Now I'd like to talk a bit about the Other Side itself. While I've tried to describe it in previous books, in all honesty it would be difficult for anyone to give it an adequate depiction, especially because there's no evil or negativity of any kind there. Just imagine . . . not only do the "big things" such as war, killing, torture, crime, and other atrocities not exist, but neither do anger, jealousy, greed, abuse, aggravation, laziness, pain, poor health, and so on.

Of course, our finite minds, which are used to this planet's continual negativity, find it impossible that any such place could or does exist. We think, *Now wait a minute—it's hard enough for two people to get along peaceably, let alone the billions who are on the Other Side.* Others might take a different tack and wonder, *If we're all so goody-goody to each other, where is the passion and emotion? Do we just become zombies who walk around smiling and offering platitudes to one another all the time?* While these are legitimate and logical viewpoints, they're based on our cynical and jaundiced earthly outlooks.

When we're Home, we utilize our minds at full capacity—we have all available knowledge at our disposal, and that knowledge (along with God) makes it a paradise. It also doesn't hurt that we are encased in perfect bodies that don't need food, drink, or rest. We're in a magnificently beautiful physical environment that's never marred by aggravations such as vermin or unpleasant weather. We can live in any domicile we choose and adjust it to our specifications in an instant just by thinking.

Lakes, rivers, forests, waterfalls, mountains, oceans, and houses in every architectural style imaginable abound on the Other Side. Just like on Earth, people have a place that they call home, which they can design and decorate to their hearts' content. Some prefer city living and dwell in spaces that are like apartments or townhouses, while others reside where there's plenty of land and privacy. Since materialism and social status are never needed on the Other Side, most homes tend to be practical yet comfortable. You won't see any hovels *or* huge mansions, as all who live in this paradise are happy and can have everything they need. It's hard to explain that human desires just don't manifest like they do on our "hell" of a planet.

Famous artists give their work away to those who love it, musicians perform for the sheer joy of playing and entertaining, and lectures are presented by prominent experts in their fields just to share knowledge. You see, there's simply no need for money or material things. While we can have them if we want, there's no value to them other than as decorative items for our homes or bodies. As we can instantly *think* ourselves to any place we want to go, vehicles are unnecessary. There's no need to eat or drink, and there is certainly no type of illness. And because we can have anything we desire, there's no crime or violence of any kind.

We can choose any work we want to do on the Other Side; therefore, we all have a passion for our vocations. We live and work together in complete harmony and teamwork in a totally peaceful and loving environment; consequently, our minds are so opened up to the truth about God that there's no need for politics or power. We're all certainly living our faith, thanks to God's overwhelming presence and love, so there's no organized religion. We enjoy recreation and the arts, wilderness and natural beauty, and good people all around whom we can interact with socially. In other words, everything we could ever conceivably want or need is at our fingertips, so negative human traits never come into play.

Since we do keep our individual personalities that have developed over our entire existence, we're not all zombies with one-track minds. If we do happen to disagree with another soul (which is a rarity), our spirituality immediately makes us understand both viewpoints, so disagreements fade off into nothingness instantaneously. Our spiritual mind, which operates at full capacity, has the capability to understand almost everything instantly and recognizes the complete and full truth that exists in creation . . . hence, a perfect environment with no evil or negativity.

If we don't care for a particular type of personality, then we probably won't run in the same social circles. We'd also know in our spiritual mind that regardless of that individual's personality, he or she is a good person, so we could (and would) interact with him or her without any problems. The Other Side is not illogical, so we do tend to revolve around people whose dispositions, beliefs, interests, and so forth are more in line with ours. Thus, interest groups tend to band together—surfer buddies hang out with each other, while scientists pal around together, but there's always the occasional person who does both. Just because someone likes the casual lifestyle of surfing doesn't mean that he or she can't also adore the study of microbes.

We all play and work hard on the Other Side because we have a passion for whatever we're doing. We are truly free to pursue any endeavor we wish, for we're not forced or pressured in any way to do something that we have no desire for. It's up to each individual to choose to do what he or she truly loves . . . and everyone at Home is doing just that!

Time and the Temples

It certainly makes sense that if we're doing all this work on the Other Side to advance our souls, then there would be physical places where it would get done. We have real and solid bodies over there, so we require desks, chairs, and other equipment, just as we need teachers, experts, counselors, and the like to help us learn. How confusing it would be to wander around trying to research or discover with no direction, or without a place designated for a particular subject of learning or occupation.

Let me stop here and tell you what I thought as I was writing about the 24 temples and halls: *For God's sake, how do we get anything else done if we have to visit all of these places?* Well, Francine assures me that there is no "time" on the Other Side, as it is more or less all converged into a singular moment in which everything is happening at the same time, so you can be in two or three places at once in your full essence (known as bi- or trilocating). I know it's hard to understand, but I'm trying to explain it in layperson's terms without your needing to be a physicist to grasp the concept. Just trust me on this one if you don't quite get it (I sure didn't for the longest time) and know that we all can bi- or trilocate on the Other Side.

Quadrants and Levels

The makeup of the Other Side can also be challenging for our limited earthly minds to comprehend. For example, it's another dimension that's superimposed on our own, about three feet above this plane. In much the same way that we don't hear a dog whistle because it's too high pitched for our human ears, the vibration of our true Home is so much higher than ours that we don't perceive it.

There are continents over there (consisting of the seven that exist here, as well as those of Atlantis and Lemuria), but each one is divided up into four sections or areas called "quadrants." Basically for the purposes of better organization and efficiency, each quadrant is then devoted to a particular level. So most of the entities that reside, say, in the fourth quadrant are also on the fourth level and have vocations that are mainly artistic in nature. Although the bulk of entities in a quadrant are on the same level, there *are* many who are on different levels residing there as well. So you might have a scientist (fifth level) who likes a pastoral setting for his home, thus he might choose to live in the third quadrant (plants and animal husbandry) where there is more open space for animals and lovely landscapes to look at.

The reason most residents of a particular quadrant are on the same level is not only to share common pursuits, but also to work together more efficiently. In other words, those drawn to marine biology (third level) would probably want to go to a quadrant where oceans and lakes exist, but it would also help them to be with others who are working in the same field for consultation and research purposes. It's more effective to be with those of like interest—and since on the Other Side we only have to think ourselves to a location to instantly be there, it's no great hardship to reside anywhere we please. Nevertheless, most of us do choose to live in the same area as those who share similar interests and vocations, which makes for a more compatible, and better organized, environment.

Let's say that we needed to get research on the elephant—well, all we'd need to do is go to the third quadrant to find scientists and experts who are well versed in that subject, as well as the elephant itself in the wild. Since the third quadrant on each continent holds almost all the animals, you can then find everything you want in one place . . . which is certainly much easier than going from place to place trying to find a particular scientist or expert. (I will explain more about this in Part II, but for a detailed look at our Home's quadrants and levels, please see my book *Exploring the Levels of Creation.*)

Again, we can also find any expert we might need in the various halls, temples, and research centers that exist in essentially the same place on the Other Side. If we took the nine continents and brought them together, the designated center would be, to use an example from our planet, around the Baja California peninsula of Mexico. (As a little aside, on the Other Side that particular area is lush and green, as are most areas that correspond to deserts on Earth.) And that's where all the great halls, temples, and research centers happen to be located. However, because we can instantaneously travel to a different place simply by thinking ourselves there, distance is never a problem. This is another benefit of having our minds at full capacity.

Help from Beyond the Veil

Since the Other Side is a thriving paradise, everyone there is aware of the trials and tribulations that those of us in incarnations on Earth have to deal with, and they're so willing to assist us whenever possible. Yet I've discovered that a lot of us have no idea how often we seek relief from the Other Side. For example, most of us take astral trips there three or four times a week, and we often communicate with that dimension in our dreams. There are many avenues of help that we can seek from beyond the veil, and these include all of its edifices.

In making you aware of these available aids, it's my wish that they will help each and every one of you face and deal with the challenges in your life more easily. Knowledge is power, and hopefully you can use this new information to keep on track and completely succeed in your own mission for God. And that's where this book comes in.

Some of the wisdom contained herein has come from the research my ministers and I have done on hypnosis regressions, astral travel, and near-death experiences. The anonymous subjects involved related what they saw and went through, and many times it was so similar that it was as if they had communicated with each other—which was impossible, as no interaction among subjects took place. Yet the bulk of what's in these pages has come from the research trance with Francine that occurred awhile back. Where appropriate, I've shared questions from members of the salon, along with her responses; I've also included stories from individuals regarding their own experiences in specific halls.

Now while the buildings on the Other Side don't necessarily fall into what we on Earth would recognize as an "organizational pattern," I've broken this book down into parts so that you can navigate your way around them more easily. In Part I, I'll introduce you to the sites that we tend to seek out when we first come through the tunnel, for they orient us to the Other Side. Then in Part II, I'll go over the temples that appeal to the different levels. And in Part III, I'll focus on the halls that we can particularly benefit from while still incarnated on this planet. (Note that some chapters contain more information and are longer than others; however, this doesn't mean that those particular locales are more important.)

You can visit your true Home whenever you want, and one of the best ways to do so is through meditation. So in Part IV, you'll find specific meditations designed to help you reach the wonderful edifices I'm about to tell you about. In this way, you can gain resolutions or reconnections or free yourself of the anxiety and other innumerable challenges that make life on Earth so miserable.

So with that in mind, it's now time to become familiar with the many temples that serve various functions on the Other Side. I really believe that you'll find this new information as fascinating as I do!

PART I

Sites That Welcome Us to the Other Side

Chapter 1

THE TEMPLE OF ORIENTATION

One of the things I love about being a Gnostic is that we're constantly finding and receiving fresh information and learning about new things. For example, I've always put forth that when we cross over to the Other Side, one of the first things we do is go to the Hall of Wisdom. Well, Francine has informed me of a slight change: Before we visit that particular building, we actually go into the Temple of Orientation.

Going through these first few halls helps us get accustomed to being back Home. My spirit guide says that the only ones who don't seem to need this process are the entities who die very young (before the age of six) because they were on the Other Side so recently that they have total recall. The longer we're incarnated on Earth, however, the more we need a full orientation. Even more important, we find that although we want to get "back in the groove" as quickly as possible, we're not really able to do so on our own.

You know how it is when you've been on a long trip and can be overwhelmed with what to do first when you get back: Do you unpack, water the plants, call your family, do the laundry, or just collapse into bed? Thankfully, on the Other Side it's all laid out for you in a well-organized plan. And everything does come back to you fairly quickly. It's much like when I traveled back to my hometown of Kansas City, Missouri, to visit my loved ones. It had been many, many years since I had been there, so I thought, *How will I get from the Plaza to my house?* But as my son and I drove down the streets, it almost immediately unfolded right before me. All of a sudden, it was, "Oh, I remember! Take Rock Hill Road to Gillam. Now go up Charlotte."

So you can see that getting around on the Other Side would be even more familiar, since you've spent an eternity there. It brings about a feeling of touching base: "Of course . . . this is my Home. I've lived here for an eternity and was just away for a while."

The Temple of Orientation glows with a soft and beautiful white light (much like the tunnel we pass through to get to and from the Other Side) and is Romanesque in design, yet it's not as ornate as you'll find some of the other halls to be. It also isn't very elaborate inside; in fact, you might even say that it's somewhat spartanly furnished compared to the other buildings we'll be exploring in this book. Its furnishings reflect its purpose—everything is all business, for this temple's very important purpose is to lessen the trauma suffered by all souls going in and out of life.

There are two large sets of double doors in the front of this edifice: one with the word *Incoming* above it and the other with the word *Outgoing*. Both sets lead to the main portion of the temple, which is very large and divided into two distinct sections: again, one for incoming souls and one for outgoing souls. From Francine's description of this central space, it seems to me that each area is like a type of auditorium, with many seats and several aisles; however, there are also small cubicles lining all sides.

If you're an incoming soul, you sit down with your guide until a counselor (orientator) comes to escort you to one of the cubicles. While you're waiting, you might notice a huge board with blinking and solid red and green lights on the wall facing you. This board is actually an indicator of incoming souls who have either passed or are close to passing: A blinking red light means that a soul is about to pass, while a solid green light notes that a soul has indeed passed over just moments ago. You might even notice your name and that the green light next to it is solid.

16

While the Temple of Orientation is always full, amazingly there's plenty of room for everyone, along with enough orientators to meet everyone's needs rapidly and efficiently. So your counselor quickly appears to escort you to a cubicle, where he or she, your guide, and you all sit down in utter privacy. Your orientator begins to talk softly to you, answering any questions you might have and reminding you that you're safe and back Home. You may still be somewhat disoriented, but memories are flooding back to you of the life you just lived and how you died. (Only a few of those who pass don't remember such details at this point.)

The counselor assures you of many things: "Yes, you did complete what you needed to learn," "No, you didn't go too soon," "Your family on Earth is all right," as well as anything else to make you more comfortable and relaxed, thus orienting you back Home. He or she knows that you may still be tied to your just-passed life and have some disorientation or confusion, thus explaining, "Remember that you'll now go to the Hall of Wisdom. You've done a good job, and it's good to have you back Home."

You find that you're much more relaxed, and the first wonderful rays of realization that you're truly Home begin to form. You suddenly feel an overpowering love that is permeating your being, and you remember that this is the love of God (which we all feel on the Other Side), which is so much more powerful than any earthly sensation. It's so magnificent—almost overpowering—and it fills your soul with such compassion that it practically shouts, "In you I am pleased!" All the last vestiges of stress and anxiety about leaving life fade away and are put to rest. You see again how young you are and how good you feel. Your body seems so much lighter, as all the gravity and heaviness of your earthly shell is gone, much like the contrast of coming out of a swimming pool and becoming aware of how heavy your body truly is.

I think it's important to mention here that the counselors who work in the Temple of Orientation have to study long and hard to prepare for this role so that they can help with an individual's chart (this is the life plan every human being plots out before incarnating on Earth). Outgoing souls have their charts pretty much set when they go to the Temple of Orientation, but counselors give them tools to help them get through it and remind them to rely on their angels; guides; and, of course, the Mother and Father God.

The orientators usually perform counseling as their only vocation because there are always souls coming in and out. What they do is crucial, for they not only have to be experts in all kinds of therapy, but they also have to know about the nuances of life and how they can affect a soul. They have to be able to pick up signs of any problems through body language, speech, behavior, or what have you. They're also the ones who decide if a soul needs to be cocooned because of trauma (I'll talk more about this later on).

While the Temple of Orientation is ever ready to help any outgoing or incoming soul, Francine says that almost all those coming in are arriving from their last lives on Earth. So are these counselors in danger of losing their jobs? Never, for there will continue to be some souls who want to go to other planets. All of these orientators can also become teachers.

After Francine described this hall in a trance in our salon, several attendees remarked, "I've seen that place!" One woman said that she knew she was a counselor. Yes, counselors or orientators do incarnate because the experience gives them a greater understanding about life on Earth and the various charts that people can create for themselves.

Another lady later told me over the phone that she'd had a dream that was akin to an astral state (which it actually was) where she was in a cubicle with low glowing lights, and a beautiful entity was explaining what she'd gone through and why. Francine says that she had definitely been in the Temple of Orientation, where she'd received some counseling.

I also had a man basically report the same thing to me, but he added that he remembered being advised about going *in* to life. He remembered the counselor holding a scroll and reading off what he called "significant bullet points" about his upcoming life: He'd have a hard entrance and a predilection for drug addiction; and he wouldn't get married until he was 30, after which he'd lose his first baby but then have a little girl. He said that the counselor had gone on and on, but he didn't remember the rest. Then he told me that in this incarnation he had indeed been a premature baby and almost died; had a bad bout with drugs in his teens; got married in his early 30s; and watched helplessly while he and his wife lost their first baby at the age of eight months . . . only to have a little boy (the only difference, it would seem) a short while later. The man said that he so wished he could remember the rest of what his counselor had told him, but I don't think he was supposed to know anything else.

Speaking of outgoing souls, after meeting with their orientators, those who are about to incarnate then go into a state of seclusion with an angel known as a "Virtue" (which I'll talk about later in this book). After that contemplative period, they're led to a glass room that's beautifully scented and illuminated by a soft purple light that then turns blue. Outgoing souls don't stay long in this room before they literally become infants, as their bodies change from those of 30-year-olds to those of newborns. This is done so that the souls can acclimate to the tiny vehicles they'll have when they come out of their mothers' wombs on Earth.

As outgoing souls are helped into waiting wombs, they begin to lose most of their conscious knowledge in the process. This happens because if they could clearly recall what the Other Side was like and what they've chosen for themselves, their test of learning would be minimized and not be as effective. Yet there's almost always some knowledge that leaks through to a degree, which explains why so many young boys and girls distinctly describe past lives or what it's like on the Other Side.

For example, when my granddaughter, Angelia, was four, she came to me and said, "Bagdah [her nickname for me], I was in this lonely place with lights and I saw all these babies who were leaving. I wanted to go in, but a pretty lady [her guide, Ariel] said, 'You can't go in there because those are souls getting ready to go into life.'" Angelia was very upset because she wanted to go into the room and play with the babies, but I let her know exactly what she'd seen. If we explain such things rationally to children, they'll understand because they've been to the Other Side so recently themselves.

Cocooning

Regardless of how we died, as I said earlier, most of us do make it to the Other Side. However, some who come over don't immediately go through the orientation process and are instead "cocooned." You see, if they've suffered extremely violent passings, some souls may become traumatized in the process, so the orientators will wrap them in warm blankets and place them in cubicles with comforting music or even soothing lights and colors. It's almost like being back in the womb but still on the Other Side. Extreme cases may be put into a deep sleep, almost like a coma, during which the orientators will deprogram the trauma incurred and give these individuals' minds some intense healing.

Most entities who are cocooned are only in that state for a month or so, but the extreme cases can be kept as such for a year or more. (Of course there's no time on the Other Side, so I'm referring to this according to our calendar.) I'm convinced that's why people often tell me that they haven't heard from passed-over loved ones who experienced a horrible demise. Interestingly, my father didn't contact me for ten months after he passed, much to my aggravation. His was not a terrible death, but Francine said that since he and I were so close, he may have carried so much grief over with him that they cocooned him. I often wish they could cocoon *us* down here when we're faced with the raw, dragonlike grief of losing a loved one.

(If you'd like to reach the Temple of Orientation through meditation, please turn to page 185 after reading the instructions on pages 181–184.)

❧ ❧ ❧

Chapter 2

THE HALL
OF WISDOM

The next site on our "tour" is the Hall of Wisdom. The very name implies that its function is to help us understand what life on this planet is about and what is to be learned from it.

Like the Temple of Orientation, the Hall of Wisdom is a huge Romanesque structure. You may wonder why so many buildings on the Other Side reflect this type of architecture. Well, it has existed for an eternity over there—so in actuality the ancient Romans (along with the Greeks, Egyptians, and members of every other civilization throughout history) duplicated what was infused to them from beyond the veil. In fact, Francine states that *everything* that is beautiful and useful on Earth first existed on the Other Side and was then infused into the minds of the appropriate architects, inventors, doctors, researchers, and scientists so that it would become a reality to benefit our world.

Anyway, the Hall of Wisdom boasts grand columns and seven white marble steps leading up to golden doors. Almost all of the temples have that number of steps before their entrances because Francine says that the numbers 7, 9, and 11 tend to repeat often on the Other Side. And like all of the sites described in this book, the Hall of Wisdom also has Latin lettering over its main portal describing its function. (The various inscriptions are more for decoration than anything, since everyone on the Other Side knows where each and every building is.) When you go inside, you notice that it's like a cathedral, with towering colonnades and a beautiful stained-glass skylight that is absolutely massive in scope. There is also a multitude of lovely white cushioned benches scattered about the enormous marble floor.

You go to sit on one of these benches when a large convex glass appears out of the floor. This apparatus is called a "scanning machine" because it shows you every aspect of your life as if on a television or movie screen. You can view each event, action, episode, and emotion of your just-lived existence in vivid color and in stereo. While you might be concerned that this process takes you almost as long to watch as it did to live, remember that there is no such thing as time on the Other Side, although it does seem to go at a faster pace, almost as if it's compressed. It's very much like how so many people say that their life "flashed" in front of them during a brush with death.

You can start and stop the scanner, take mental notes, and see how well you dealt with a particular situation or what the best possible way to handle it would have been (almost like a perfect-solution scenario). Because, although your life was charted, everything depends on your outlook and what you learned. You can then decide if you want to come back into life and experience something that you left undone.

Usually we pick the number of lives we hope we'll learn from, but since we want to gain even more knowledge or feel a calling, we often take on what we call "example" or "option" lives. It's somewhat like planning to go to college for four years but then deciding to keep on going for our master's instead. Free will only exists on the Other Side, so once we incarnate, we're bound by the contract we made with God. We're so aware of this at Novus Spiritus that when something happens to us that's funny, sad, or unbelievable, we say, "Flag that." This refers to the fact that we know our lives are being recorded, so to speak; and when we get to the Other Side we'd like to have our friends and loved ones scan the event with us so they can laugh, cry, or have a real recognition of how we handled that situation. (Now when I say "cry," it's more metaphorical because there's no sadness on the Other Side—it really means being empathetic.)

Francine has often told me that we're too hard on ourselves during this scanning process, so counselors sometimes come in and point out the good things we've done and how much we learned, even though it was painful. I have many clients who feel that they're off track or have lost their way, but in the majority of cases, this is far from the truth. The fact is that sometimes when things are difficult, we're really learning our themes or lessons for life . . . whether it's tolerance, temperance, responsibility, patience, or the like. As I told one woman, if life was all great we wouldn't (and shouldn't) be down here because this planet is our school.

Taking the book of Genesis metaphorically, how else would we find out anything unless we bit into the so-called apple of knowledge? God says that we have to go down and till the field and bear our children in sorrow; therefore, if we expect to come here and have an undisturbed life full of joy and no sadness, we're in the wrong place to learn.

Now as you scan and go over different parts of your life, God's voice doesn't echo through the hall and tell you how bad you were. *You* are the only one who can judge you. Since your mind is at full capacity on the Other Side, you're like a miniature God and carry His understanding. You know the good you've done, the stupid things you've done, and on and on it goes.

With experience comes knowledge, and with knowledge comes wisdom. So if you've hurt someone needlessly, you can release it, knowing that you've learned from it. Whatever you do, don't get too caught up worrying about karma. It's true that everything is written, but it's *how you handle it* that's important. If you get wrapped up in guilt, especially when you didn't mean to hurt someone, you've got to let it go . . . after all, others have to learn, too, and it was all written in their charts as well.

I had a very dark-souled mother, for instance. I took care of her until the day she died, but as time went on, my patience ran pretty thin with her. Will I dwell on the times that I got short-tempered? No, because I'm human and she *was* a handful. (Also, although I don't say this with any measure of joy, I did learn to be a better mother because of her.) So if you're carrying some unfounded guilt, realize that you'll get rid of it on the Other Side.

After you're done scanning your just-lived life, then you'll take some time to meditate and contemplate what you've been through so far. It's like one long book of existence, with each life or chapter adding to the next—all of your trials and tribulations, as well as your joys, have brought you to this point of spirituality. During this time, you truly commune with our Creators because the Hall of Wisdom has an energy that gives you the knowledge and understanding of your own spiritual standing. Mother and Father God assure you in the most dear and personal way that Their love for you is everlasting. More than ever before, you understand what Jesus meant when he said that the temple of God is within. While there's a Divine kingdom on the Other Side, the more your *own* kingdom expands, the more you're able to give love, loyalty, and commitment to our Creators.

(If you'd like to reach this temple through meditation, please turn to page 187 after reading the instructions on pages 181–184.)

Chapter 3

THE HALL
OF JUSTICE

The Hall of Justice is the sanctuary where the revered Council of Elders meets to advise all those in need. It's the smallest of the three main temples (the Halls of Wisdom, Justice, and Records) that are grouped together and built in a Romanesque theme, with large entrance pillars and grand golden domes. However, the Hall of Justice has two distinguishing features: (1) a very impressive and treasured statue of the Mother God, Azna, at its entrance; and (2) illustrious gardens.

The representation of Azna is both glorious in beauty and awesome in scope. Standing perhaps 50 feet high, it shows our Mother in all Her regal glory, and it is surrounded by beautiful fountains that augment the craftsmanship so evident in the sculpture. The statue depicts the Mother God in full battle regalia (a metaphorical expression of Her constant fight against negativity and evil), with shining armor covering Her bosom and torso and armored leggings up to Her knees. Azna carries a magnificent sword in Her left hand that's pointed toward the ground, while Her right arm is lifted up as if urging Her Thrones (Her army of angels) onward. Her head is uncovered; Her hair is in a long, hanging braid; and Her resplendent and commanding face shows an expression of extreme determination. This likeness is meant to convey our

Mother's continuing intervention to defeat evil at every turn . . . and it certainly gets its message across.

The famous gardens of the Hall of Justice are arguably the finest cultivated grounds on the Other Side. They are quite massive, covering hundreds of acres that contain paths, benches, alcoves, niches, ponds, waterfalls, footbridges, creeks, fountains, and the like; along with a dazzling array of flowers, bushes, and trees of every conceivable type or species that you could imagine. In God's perfect environment beyond the veil, there's no need for gardening maintenance of any kind, but horticulturists flock to tend to and expand these particular grounds with their own hands. They prefer to do all the menial work themselves; in addition, they enjoy making continual changes and expansions and performing experimental work on the thousands of different species of flora. To these "plant people," it's the greatest of joys, and those who stroll through the gardens are always met with the smiling faces of those who maintain them.

These grounds are for everyone to enjoy, whether it's just for a nice and easy ramble or a more meditative exercise in some alcove or shrine area. They're so extensive that visitors feel as if they're alone within the gardens no matter where they go, yet little animals and birds also live there peacefully. Therefore, visitors almost always end up interacting with them in some small, happy way . . . usually with a group of creatures surrounding them or in their laps. Squirrels, monkeys, chipmunks, rabbits, pygmy deer, and the like—along with birds that defy description, including gorgeous parrots of every vivid color in the rainbow—are continually found happily cavorting together or with visitors. This area is truly one of the most magnificent places on the Other Side.

The Council

Along with being a very beautiful building with awe-inspiring grounds, the Hall of Justice also serves as the convening place for the Council of Elders, a group of highly evolved entities or "special creations" from God. Most commonly called "the Council," the

Elders are also known as "the Brotherhood," "the White Brotherhood," and "the Master Teachers," although this last term is something of a misnomer because they're actually the Master Teachers *of* the many Master Teachers on the Other Side.

Council members don't tend to look like they're 30 years old; rather, most of them have white or graying hair (and, in the case of males, long beards), which is why they're referred to as "Elders." Their appearance is symbolic in nature, as age does tend to be associated with wisdom, but it also distinguishes them at a glance from the rest of the inhabitants of the Other Side. In addition, all members wear a gold medallion around their necks to designate their stature. This is mainly an "ornament of office," if you will, but it does help set apart the few on the Council who choose not to take an older visage.

Now it's always hard for those of us on this planet to relate to a perfect environment, and just as hard for me to try to explain it in writing. Even if we seem to have a wonderful life here on Earth, we still have problems surrounding us—even if they're what most people would consider to be petty nuisances. All of us here have challenges of one sort or another, and not a day goes by in which we don't face them, so it can be difficult to understand or even imagine a place in which there are no problems of any kind . . . yet that's truly what the Other Side is like.

The function of the Council is just what its name implies: Members never judge but are always there for those who seek help of any kind. However, since there's no negativity or evil over there, the only advice anyone requires is directly related to the negative plane or school we know as Earth. In other words, the only ones on the Other Side who actually need counseling are those who are entering an incarnation, coming from a recent incarnation, in the midst of an incarnation, or the spirit guides of those who are incarnated.

If you have a problem that can't be resolved in the Temple of Orientation, you take your concerns to the Council, which has been aware of your name, soul, and chart for eternity. When you consider how many billions of entities there are on the Other Side, it's amazing that they know so much about you. This shows you that the Elders really are God's "special creations," or emissaries who have vast knowledge, sympathy, and spiritual understanding far beyond what we could ever know or comprehend on this planet.

It's interesting to note that the Council does have a hierarchy, which is revealed in how they sit at their table when they convene. Their table is square-shaped and open on one end, and the head of the Council sits opposite of the middle of the open portion, with other members gathering in descending rank on both his right and left sides. Where a member sits has more to do with honor than anything relating to his or her power, although Francine says that the head of the Council does exert great influence on its guidance and decisions. (By the way, she tells me his name is Malachi and he's a wonderfully kind and wise man.) She notes that there are 22 Elders at the present time, and the number for all practical purposes doesn't change.

If you feel that something is unfinished or unjust, the Council can be of great assistance to you. You'd go over your issue with the members and even invite them to scan your life with you if you so choose, but they always respect the privacy between you and God. Your guide is also in attendance and helps to explain the reasons why you did what you did (without offering excuses). You then have the opportunity to look back over what happened to see if you could have handled it with more grace, less guilt, more courage, fewer cross words, or what have you; and this doesn't disturb the major highway of your chart. Perhaps you stayed too long at one stop or should have speeded up at another . . . you got where you had to go, but being human, you probably did make things far more difficult than they should have been.

My grandmother used to say, "Lazy people take the most pains." I've seen that so often in my own life when I try to make something easier and end up making it twice as hard for myself. Sure, I get it done, but I often think of how great things would have been if I would have simply exerted the effort and done it right (and more quickly) in the first place.

The Elders will also quell your fears about some occurrence that was nightmarish and explain why your chart took you there and why you did such and such. In other words, they help you justify your existence and actions. Members of the Council answer your queries and truly *counsel* you. They make no judgments and don't make you feel guilty in any way, but rather pointedly ask questions in order to assist you. For example, they're almost sure to ask if you would have handled a particular situation differently; and, if so, what you would have done instead. Then the Elders will show you the outcome if you would have chosen a so-called different road. While almost any path you choose keeps you on track, some are filled with more hardships than others.

Let's say that your chart indicates you'll have children but you wait until much later in life to do so and find that it's really difficult on you emotionally or even physically. While you finished the race, so to speak, you've become awfully worn out in the process. So while you did fulfill your chart, you could have done it in a way that would have been easier on yourself. You may view this as being off track, but it isn't.

It's very hard in the human time frame to hit the mark every time, and we also find that timing can be difficult to gauge. How often have we said, "It was like a miracle—everything fell into place like it was planned"? Conversely, we can also find ourselves in situations where whatever could go wrong did. We got so distracted, for instance, that we ended up missing our plane; or we found our normal parking lot full, which caused us to be late for an important meeting. Of course since this is all a learning process, we often sabotage ourselves so that we can gain some knowledge—be it patience, tolerance, survival, endurance, or the simple fact that we have to slow down and get our priorities straight.

The Council will try to create justice in all aspects of our lives—and what's even more important, keep us from creating excessive karma for ourselves. How many times do we know that a situation is hopeless but we keep on beating ourselves up to make it right? We stay in the same place or circumstance longer than we need to and suffer needlessly. We've learned and *over*learned our lesson, so we don't have to victimize ourselves by hanging on and creating havoc, illness, and depression in our lives.

Even if we did happen to go off track, this wonderful Council helps us see why we did so and then asks the all-important questions: "Do you want to take on another life under similar circumstances and try to do better? Or would you rather work it out here [on the Other Side]?" Now this is by no means the only reason why we live other lives, but it does happen. Most of the time, of course, we take on further incarnations because we want to learn for God.

It's true that if we don't knock on the door, it won't open . . . but what's even more important is to know which door to knock on. So as I've said many times (and might say again), as we visit these temples on the Other Side, it proves God's omnipotent presence over and over, as well as how many of His entities are gathered to help us knock on the right doors for help.

Again, the amazing thing is that we always thought one had to die to access these halls, but through Francine—along with my research group's work in dreams, hypnosis regression, and astral travel—we've discovered that people have found themselves inside their walls for years and felt much better afterward. A few have even named these buildings, while others described them but didn't know exactly where they were, other than that they were in these amazing structures where they were given great solace and comfort. Often individuals remembered these experiences after they had awakened from sleep, come out of hypnosis or an astral state, or even had a near-death experience.

For example, I recently had a client tell me, "Sylvia, I wasn't asleep, but rather in a meditative state, when all of a sudden I found myself in this Romanesque building. I was surrounded by these beautiful, glowing entities sitting at a squarish, three-sided table. I was standing in the middle of them and discussing a facet of my life that I wanted clarification on. I don't remember them speaking with their mouths, but I did get the message that I should leave my abusive husband or I would find myself not necessarily off course, but putting myself through more hell than I needed to."

In other words, this woman said that she was told she'd already learned her lesson, so it was time to move on. I've heard variations on this theme so many times.

Another time a man I was doing a regression with began to talk about a life in England where he was a guard in a prison out on a lonely moor, and he ended up dying of tuberculosis. He saw himself going through the tunnel and found himself in the Hall of Wisdom, where he scanned many lives. I directed him to see anything that bothered him, and he became visibly distressed—he started to cry and stated that he'd been unbearably cruel to the prisoners. I said that he could always go back to the scanner but wondered if there was any other place he could find peace with respect to this issue. He immediately found himself in the Hall of Justice, in front of the three-sided table with beautiful entities seated around it. He even felt that there was a guide or angel standing to his right (which is, in fact, what they do). Through more tears, he related that he could barely watch how far his cruelty had gone with these prisoners.

My client then stated in a very low, meditative voice what the Elders were saying, almost as if he were repeating a litany. He said that in no way did they condone his behavior, but they knew that he'd felt like a prisoner himself. His wife had died of pneumonia, so he had to raise four children on his own with hardly any money coming from this horrific job. He'd become mentally ill in the process, which didn't totally excuse what he'd done but did give him some insight into his cruelty. My client said that he had two lives left to live and at some point really wanted to come back in and be imprisoned so that he'd know what it felt like. He'd charted a life in which he'd be put in jail, and now he knew why—and he was relieved that he'd be given the chance to "round out" what he'd done.

Members of the Council never recommended anything to my client; instead, they simply pointed out some of the reasons for his behavior. Yet when he came out of the hypnosis, he was just beaming. (I don't know if I'd be so happy at the prospect of prison in any life.) He explained that this regression had really helped him understand his disdain for authority and a claustrophobic condition that was so severe that if he ever felt penned in, he became quite violent. Once it had gotten so bad at a restaurant, where he was in a booth and tables were crowded in around him, that in his panic and anger he had overturned some of the furniture. Of course he was very quickly escorted out and was told that he was lucky the police weren't called . . . and that he was never to return to that establishment.

One year later, my client wrote me a beautiful letter telling me that his anger was now totally under control. He felt more spiritual or, as he put it, more "finished." I knew what he meant: He'd come full circle, and it was really all thanks to the help of the Council at the Hall of Justice. I still wouldn't be thrilled about a life behind bars, but it certainly didn't seem to bother him.

Now realize that this man *did* have a choice. After understanding what he did, he could have essentially made it up by doing good works on the Other Side or coming back to live a life in which he would be a prisoner. This again shows that our free-will choice is made on the Other Side, not on Earth. Once we're in life, the die is pretty well cast.

As you go through these temples, you're going to develop a deeper meaning of spirituality and the greatness of our Creators and Their mercy. Not only are we never, ever left alone down here, but even in our total bliss on the Other Side, we can still iron out all the difficulties we've had in our existences. All the varying aids and means of support that God has laid in place—such as the Council; the various buildings where help can be sought and given; and the myriad entities who serve as spirit guides, counselors, teachers, and orientators—are there to help us while we're in and out of life.

For example, people have told me that to merely stand before the Council is one of the holiest moments of all, as well as a healing experience they'll never forget. I have clients who go back many times just to feel that great love and empathy, as well as the sensation that they're the most important people in the world, which is what being in the presence of the Elders is like.

Remember that you can get help from the Council at any time during this life, rather than waiting until you die; so if you're in confusion about your chart, before you go to sleep at night ask God to let you go to the Hall of Justice and get advice from the Council of Elders. (Or, if you'd like to reach this temple through meditation, please turn to page 191 after reading the instructions on pages 181–184.)

please turn to page 191 after reading the instructions on pages 181–184.

Chapter 4

THE HALL
OF RECORDS

CARDIFF
CAERDYDD

The next temple we'll visit is the one in which all the data on every person and thing ever created can be found. The Hall of Records sits to the left of the Hall of Wisdom and shares a similar architectural style, with many huge columns surrounding its entire perimeter and an immense towering dome on its roof. As it is the largest structure on the Other Side, the building itself is absolutely gigantic in scope—it houses miles and miles of corridors containing seemingly endless shelves and storage areas with every kind of book, disk, tape, chip, and scroll imaginable, along with high-tech devices that haven't even been invented in our world as yet.

The Hall of Records (or what many psychics or mediums refer to as the "Akashic Records") contains the minutiae of every entity's existence, including its beginning, its life on the Other Side, all its incarnations on Earth and other planets, and so on. You might say that it's impossible to store that amount of material in one building, and under normal circumstances, using earthly physics, you'd be right. Yet despite the seemingly finite parameters of this temple's exterior, its interior actually seems to take up a different amount of space, which is as large as it needs to be.

A physicist friend of mind once tried to explain this concept to me, calling it "nonlocal reality." I understood it to mean that everything is happening all at once; therefore, there *is* no time or space. A lightbulb went off in my head at the time, for this was exactly what I'd been writing and talking about for years, only I'd always called it "God's now."

Now one of the interesting things about the Hall of Records and its storage system is that certain knowledge—such as all the books and other written material human beings have created since their inception—are stored in such a way that any subject or document that has ever existed can be instantly brought up in numerous ways, such as by simply speaking a word or even emanating a thought. But the most intriguing part of this is that any of the records having to do with lives (that is, our charts) aren't stored on high-tech devices but are kept on beautiful scrolls written in Aramaic, which is the language we all read, speak, and use on the Other Side.

The Hall of Records is basically divided into two distinct areas, with general information catalogued in multiple sections much like in a library, while lives and charts are kept on scrolls in a completely different part of the building. Then there are the two extremely fascinating living-record sections: While almost impossible for us on Earth to comprehend, a "living record" is essentially a device that looks like a large enclosed area with a mammoth TV screen projecting images that surround the viewer in all directions, and it's capable of projecting a moment-by-moment detailed account of what's going on in creation. It's a memory bank of everything that has ever happened, and it constantly updates itself as new things are being created.

What's really amazing is that you can go to any point in history and actually place yourself in the middle of the action. That is, you can step right into whatever they bring up on the screen, experiencing what those in that time did, almost as if you were a ghost. So you can push a button and go back into the Civil War, for instance, and feel what fighting for the North or South was *really* like. As Francine says, "It's all around you"—you feel like you're actually living it.

I'm sure that visiting the living records is how spirit guides get the true slant on history, for they see what goes on firsthand, without having to wade through someone else's jaundiced view of it. I do remember one time in college, however, when I was doing a research paper on Alexander the Great, and Francine got a little *too* close to the action. She must have gone in too quickly or overshot her mark because she found herself in the middle of a horrendous battle, with blood and stabbings and dust and horses' hooves everywhere. There was no way she could have been hurt, but she said the whole experience was very disconcerting because it was so real.

Now if we wanted to know about Abraham Lincoln's entire life, we could indeed view it. Again, it might feel as if that would take years, but my guide says we could see a whole life in what might be an hour and a half in our time. I had this vision of a fast-forward blur of vision and action, but she assured me that it's very distinct and sequential. There are definitely parts of these lives that are considered private, though. A person's intimate moments are what they call "domed," which in our language would be akin to censoring things. (I find this to be a relief, since there are certainly parts of my life that I'm not so proud of and wouldn't want publicly exposed.) Even some horrendous crimes are told of but not shown due to their gruesome nature. So here again we see God's knowledge and mercy in enabling us to see only what we can handle.

While the living-record scanner is like having history right at your disposal, the scanner in the charts section is usually used for what its name implies. So, just like the similar machines in the Hall of Wisdom, you can look at all your past lives on this scanner. I think it would be so fascinating to do this, and when I go back Home I'd like to see my existences in Kenya, Mongolia, or any of the other places I've spent time. I want to know what the level of my spirituality was, how I handled certain situations, and even who shared my lives with me . . . so I can better understand who I am and who I've always been. Yet Francine says that many on the Other Side don't care to do this exercise—perhaps they simply can't bear to view their old pain and trauma again, which I suppose is understandable.

Many people still on Earth have successfully visited the Hall of Records, but they've never been able to read their own charts. This validates that no one, not even a psychic like me, can read his or her own chart. Oh sure, we can have premonitions and insights due to our charts being in our subconscious memory, but we can't have *conscious* memory of them. This means that only those with permission (such as our spirit guides) can read our charts, thus ensuring privacy. If we don't want our charts read, then they won't be able to be accessed.

Before I appear on Montel Williams's show, he generally tells the audience what I've been advising for years: "If you don't want to hear the answer, then don't ask the question." That's because the moment an inquiry is placed, permission is given to access your chart to get the resolution. True psychics would never get into someone's chart without permission, and I've never tried it (nor would I). I do find it funny that the predictions I make with respect to celebrities I haven't met tend to be very general compared to those I've interacted with.

I'm reminded of a regression I did on a woman named Marianne, who'd had a life in Salem, Massachusetts, and found herself planted right in the middle of the witch hunts and trials. Her name had been Elizabeth, and she'd been an herbalist (in this life she also dealt in herbs and nutrition) and thus had been hunted as a witch, although she'd managed to escape to a wooded area in New York. After traveling so many miles, her immune system had broken down, so she'd lived out the next ten years as a sickly recluse. (In this life she suffered from chronic fatigue syndrome.)

She next found herself going through the white light and to the Hall of Wisdom, where she scanned her life. She was then guided to a place where beautiful entities sat around a square table that was open at one end, and they directed her to the Hall of Records so that she could look up her chart in order to get a better understanding of her experiences. (Of course this could not be done until the life was over because we can't read our own charts when we're incarnated. But when that existence is over, everything is available so that we can learn from it.)

My client found herself in front of rows and rows of scrolls, but she couldn't tell one from another. She then heard a woman's voice calling out, "Over here, Elizabeth, it's over here!" Marianne/Elizabeth indeed discovered her scroll; after reading it, she felt that she'd lived a good life even though it had been hard and lonely and full of harsh survival.

As I've mentioned, my ministers and I always record every hypnosis regression session, so Marianne took her tape home with her. The next day I came into the office to hear that Marianne had frantically called twice wanting to see me. When she got to my office, she played me what she wanted me to hear without saying a word. Sure enough, it was the tape of her regression—and when she was in the Hall of Records, a sweet melodic voice said, "Over here, Elizabeth, it's over here!" It was so distinct that it was as if someone had been in the room with Marianne and me during our session.

Francine said this was definitely a case where my client's spirit guide was helping her find her chart, and her voice had come through on the tape. Now that was something in and of itself—but what was even more exciting was that the guide's voice came through at a time when she was looking for *Elizabeth's* chart on the Other Side, at the very same time that Marianne was in the midst of a past-life regression in her present life! If this doesn't confirm that all things are happening at once in God's now, then I don't know what could. Think about this: Marianne was in the middle of a past-life regression that was being recorded, and the recording also picked up a voice from the Other Side . . . at a time when Marianne *was* on the Other Side looking for her chart from another life! She was simultaneously being regressed and looking for records at Home, which the tape absolutely proved.

Francine says that this type of occurrence is very, very rare but will happen from time to time. Somehow a slippage occurred between the two dimensions, and the laws of physics converged with the nonlocal reality that was manifested during Marianne's regression—showing both her existence as Marianne in a hypnotic state *and* her past life as Elizabeth. Again, this goes to show that our understanding of physics here on Earth is just the tip of the iceberg as far as *true* reality is concerned.

This also proves to me that the veil between this life and the Other Side is thinning. The more the world accepts that there is another dimension, then the easier it will be for helpers to get in or make themselves known—spirit guides will be able to communicate more efficiently with their charges, and angels will be able to protect and heal better.

As an aside, it's important to point out that our spirit guides call on angels for protection and healing when we need them; in fact, we all have varying (designated) amounts of angels around us all the time for protection. As we don't need a guide or angels on the Other Side, once they help us through orientation, our designated angels then go on to another entity who needs them, and our guides can get back to their lives on the Other Side. Both spirit guides and angels are the unsung heroes who help us in life, yet while angels have distinct phyla that perform different functions, spirit guides have only one purpose: to help us make it through our incarnations and learn our lessons with as much success and as little failure as possible.

Your guide can help you with your own chart and those of others, but even he or she can't tell you everything because you have to learn it for yourself. Also, it's not always possible to read the charts of people who are closest to you, especially when it comes to those areas that affect you directly, but as time goes on and the veil gets thinner, you'll be able to read more and more. Be patient and realize that if you can't access someone's entire chart, it's because you're not meant to know the information.

Yet if you're having a terrible time with a spouse, child, or friend, you might as well try to access this person's chart, for you may indeed find out what's causing the friction between you. In the case of a woman who attended one of my salons, for instance, she went into the Hall of Records and pulled out the chart of her son, who was having a difficult time with drugs. She saw what had happened to him in a past life and was able to understand that he'd felt abandoned. This woman was always so convinced that she'd done something to cause her son's problem, and she was greatly relieved to find out that it wasn't her fault at all. She was able to get her son some help, and he ended up recovering from his addiction.

Going to the Hall of Records to find out about your loved one can be a wonderful experience. (You're not being nosy because you won't be able to see anything private.) I've even had people do "background checks" on their families; that is, they've actually been able to find missing genealogical pieces. And I believe that psychics tune in to the Akashic Records and the individual charts of people when they predict future events or happenings. As you can see, the Hall of Records is quite a helpful and fascinating place!

(If you'd like to reach this temple through meditation, please turn to page 195 after reading the instructions on pages 181–184.)

❧ ❧ ❧

Chapter 5

THE HALL
OF RESOLUTION

After three chapters discussing temples that I've written about in other books, I now return to those that are new to me, beginning with the Hall of Resolution.

According to Francine, there are a number of buildings that stand in a sort of semicircle pattern that "greet" most of us when we pass over. This particular area is one of the main focal points of the Other Side, not only for incoming souls but for residents as well. In fact, it might even be called the "heart" of our Home.

The Hall of Resolution is located near the Hall of Records, and it's fairly large and again Romanesque in style, with huge pillars at the entrance. Its entryway is lined in gold and leads to a big oval-shaped room with beautiful marble floors. Inside is an ornate table that seats six to eight people—this is set up specifically for counseling, and anyone who goes there for assistance will receive it. In fact, this temple was created to help people resolve specific issues and carryovers from their existences.

For example, let's say you've just passed over from life and have gone to the previous four temples, yet you still weren't able to resolve a particular problem. (Maybe it had to do with drugs, an abortion, or some indiscretion that you couldn't seem to come to terms with.) Even though you'd gone to the Hall of Wisdom and scanned your life and then visited the Hall of Justice to speak with the Council, you still needed more aid. In a case like this, you'd go to the Hall of Resolution and be met by a smaller group of Elders from the Council, who would then help you resolve all the hurts, defeats, phobias, and the like that you'd picked up in your last incarnation.

You'd be shown your chart to see where you might have gone off track, but you'd also be assured that you did get right back on. This counseling is intimate and very specific in nature, and it always brings resolution to whatever concerns you might have. And if you ultimately decide that you need another life to complete what you've chosen to learn, you'd receive warm and loving assistance as you deal with that as well.

Now what's especially interesting to think about is how many times you may have gone to bed with a seemingly insurmountable problem, hoping or praying that you'd find your way out of it, only to wake up in the morning and discover that the answer is right there in front of you. Well, chances are that you visited the Hall of Resolution while still on the Earth plane.

I had a period in my own life, for instance, when I was in such dire financial straits—facing IRS problems, bankruptcy, you name it—that I was half crazy. I'd be up nights pacing the floor and wringing my hands . . . not because I cared that much about the material things, but because I was worried about taking care of my family, staff, and foundation.

One night I managed to get to sleep and found myself in a place I vaguely remembered, probably because I'd been there before in other lives (even in this one), yet I didn't recall it until I was there again. As I was standing in this majestic room, I noticed a tall male entity who glowed so brightly that it was hard to distinguish his features. After conferring with the rest of the entities at the table, he stood up and addressed me in a most melodious voice. I'll never forget what he said: "Sylvia, go back into your bedroom, open your hands, and ask God to take it all. And when all has gone, remember that you still have earning power . . . within two years you will build back. It will be hard, but you will pay everything off and be better than you have ever been."

I woke up with a start, but I knew what I had to do. It took me two agonizing days to totally give up my will and truly mean it. It was one of the hardest things I've ever done because the doubt would creep in: *Sure, I can work, but how will I ever climb over this insurmountable mountain of bills?* Finally, I was able to go into my bedroom and say, "God, take it all"—and I absolutely meant it. Sometimes we have to get down into the darkest of holes before we truly surrender, but how marvelous it can be just to be able to do so.

Almost immediately after this occurrence, my house was foreclosed on, and I had to move my youngest son, my ailing and aging parents, and two staff members (who were trying to help me out) to an apartment building. We had a garage sale and made just enough to get us all settled, and I began to travel up and down the West Coast doing readings. I still had a huge clientele, but I felt better on the road at the time; besides, I could get to people who couldn't get to me. Sure enough, in a little over two years I paid the IRS the back taxes I owed, along with practically eliminating that mountain of bills. I wanted, and got, a clean slate.

I often wonder if things would have turned out so well if I hadn't surrendered my will. Now I won't lie to you—those were very hard and often discouraging years, and sometimes it felt that each day just crept by, yet I never let it affect my work. As my staff will tell you, I can be sick, grieving, or just plain down, but my ability goes on in spite of whatever is happening in my life. It's as if my gift is in a separate compartment . . . thank God!

After Francine first described this temple in our salon, many people wrote to tell me about their own experiences there. For example, I received a letter from someone who was having a terrible time with her 20-year-old daughter. Nothing this woman could do was right, for the girl was surly, spent money like water, wouldn't work, and would lock herself in her room for days. My client wrote that she'd thought of using "tough love" with her daughter, but before she did so she meditated about going to the

Hall of Resolution. She was then addressed by a beautiful being that she described as female, who told her that her daughter had a mental disorder and should immediately be taken to a doctor. The entity was even specific enough to tell my client to go to a neurologist.

When the woman came out of her meditation, she did just that. It turns out that the girl had a brain tumor, which was removed and found to be benign. My client now has a loving daughter who is enjoying a normal life and even attending nursing school.

I also heard from a man named Robert who stated that he was working 12 to 14 hours a day as a financial advisor, which was causing his health and marriage to suffer. He said that he tried to get to the Hall of Resolution for almost two weeks by asking every night, until he finally came upon the most beautiful room he'd ever seen. (According to his description, it was the same place I'd been to—it's so interesting that without knowing the particulars, all of these people came up with similar depictions and stories.) As a male clad in brilliant garments stood up to speak to Robert, my client felt angels surrounding him. He was then told by this entity that when he woke up he was to immediately quit his job and start investing in real estate. Robert indeed did both things and said that both his health and marriage were now great.

Another man wrote to tell me that anything relating to water paralyzed him with fear—he couldn't go near it, cross bridges over it, or even wade in a pool—and it was getting worse. His wife, who had been feeling neglected and didn't know about his phobia, asked him to go on a cruise in the hopes of saving their marriage. She wanted this more than anything, yet my client was so sick with fear and dread that he couldn't sleep. He used meditation to try to reach the Hall of Resolution, but he actually went into an astral state and found himself in front of several members of the Council. He wrote that he didn't remember saying anything, but understood that they knew what he was there for.

My client was told that he'd drowned in two previous lives. In one he'd belonged to a Mafia-type gang in Sicily, and he'd told on them to the authorities. He was subsequently caught by members of the gang and held under water until he drowned. In the other life, he'd been a boy in the South, and he and a bunch of child-hood friends had gone to the lake that they always swam in during the summer. They all dove in, but my client had somehow gotten caught on an old cypress root in the water. No matter how much he struggled, he'd remained trapped . . . and he'd felt such agonizing panic before he ultimately succumbed to his watery grave.

The Elders explained to this man that although he'd had these two very traumatic endings, he had nothing to fear because he wasn't charted to die by drowning in his current life. He woke up feeling completely at peace, and he was able to go on the cruise with his wife, during which he had a wonderful time.

Now while a hypnotist can help you release past-life fears with regression, I realize that you can't always get to one. (While we're on the subject, be careful of those who have no accreditation or certificate showing that they've put in the necessary hours of training. They should also have a business license.) So you can do it yourself with self-hypnosis or the meditations in Part IV; or you can just ask God, your guide, or your angels to take you to the Hall of Resolution. Many people have done this before going to bed, and they've woken up in the morning with almost magical solutions to their problems.

Dark Entities

Switching gears here, I'd like to tell you about another woman who wrote to me recently. She explained that she'd suffered from tremendous guilt because she couldn't manage to get through to her son, who seemed to hate her. By meditating, she successfully reached the Hall of Resolution the first time she tried. While there, she was told by a beautiful entity that nothing her son did was her fault, for he was a very dark soul whom she had to divorce herself from even though he was her child. This entity went on to tell her that although my client had picked this experience to learn from, she shouldn't carry any responsibility for her son's choices because they were his to make.

She wrote that even though it was very difficult, she was gradually able to separate herself from this miserable son. It hurt for a while, but she understood that it was all for the best and that she could learn from it spiritually. She said she still felt an emptiness inside, but she now also had more peace than she'd had since he was born. Not long after this happened, she learned that her son was in jail—but in some strange way, it made her feel better to know that he couldn't hurt anyone where he was.

Now for the finite mind's understanding, dark entities were initially created as good by God, but they chose to become evil. (The story of Lucifer being a fallen angel is an analogy of this process.) Such souls wreak havoc, discord, depravity, and evil; and then they perpetuate all that on Earth. Yet in a strange way we need them, for they create the negativity that all of us must work through in order to perfect and expand our souls.

Dark entities are never allowed to get to the Other Side; instead, they go back into incarnation after incarnation by passing through what I call the "left door" instead of the tunnel after death. You might ask, "Why aren't they just destroyed?" Well, Father and Mother God love all of Their creations, so They would never destroy any part of them. However, since the Earth plane is basically a school that most of us incarnate in to learn from, it will eventually be absorbed by Father God when all "white entities" have finished their education. When evil is no longer part of the "curriculum," dark entities will no longer be needed and will also be absorbed by Him.

Unfortunately, evil and negativity are in abundance on our planet for the foreseeable future, so we'll continue to be subjected to the darkness in order to learn. Now learning about all this does not make us evil—it actually does just the opposite because it shows us what *not* to do or be. In fact, many brave white entities choose to become parents to dark entities to learn for themselves, as well as to perpetuate the negative environment that helps the rest of us perfect.

It's important to keep in mind, though, that you'll never be able to change the behavior of these dark souls. I call them "heat-seeking missiles" because they're just bent on destruction. The hard thing is to have dark entities in the family and not have your own behavior influenced by them—and I know what I speak of, as my own mother was a very dark soul. And it can be especially difficult for parents because they have a tendency to love their children no matter what their behavior may be.

I hope that this has helped you understand why evil exists on Earth, and that you realize that what awaits all of us after this learning phase is over is the pure and eternal paradise of the Other Side.

(If you'd like to reach the Hall of Resolution through meditation, please turn to page 197 after reading the instructions on pages 181–184.)

(If you'd like to reach the Hall of Resolution through meditation, please turn to page 197 after reading the instructions on pages 181–184.)

❦ ❦ ❦

Chapter 6

THE HALL OF REMEMBRANCE

The Hall of Remembrance is not as large as the other temples, yet it shares their Romanesque style of architecture. It's not to be confused with the Hall of Resolution, where, as we learned in the last chapter, we can go to deal with the fears, phobias, or other issues that trouble us. Rather, this marvelous round-shaped building helps us with what we might call "behavioral overlays," or the things that we may not even be aware of yet almost feel karmically responsible for. The Hall of Resolution is where the pieces of life's puzzles are understood, or where we drop our baggage, so to speak. So to understand why we're afraid of water or have a fear of dogs, we'd go to the Hall of Resolution, but we'd visit the Hall of Remembrance in order to pull negative behavior out by its root.

When you go into this temple, you're usually struggling with a particular fault that's aggravating you, for it will help you address the behavioral aspects that you might want to change in yourself. Let's say, for instance, that you have an addiction to cigarettes, alcohol, illegal drugs, or even pharmaceutical pills such as Vicodin, codeine, OxyContin, and the like. Yes, celebrities get hooked on prescription drugs for pain and amphetamines because of busy schedules or to maintain weight and appearance, but they certainly aren't the only ones. The United States has become a drug society, and statistics now say that four out of ten people are using unneeded controlled substances, be they legal or illegal. And from what I've seen, that figure is far too low.

Most of us are probably dependent on *something,* even if it isn't necessarily harmful. For example, my big vice has always been coffee—I used to drink it all day, especially when I was teaching. I have to admit that I've had to cut way down on it, now only having four cups a day and relying more on tea. Many other intuitives have become addicted to alcohol, probably due to their stressful lives. I've been very grateful that alcohol in any form makes me sick because I've always been afraid of not being in control of my mind or of compromising my psychic abilities.

In the Hall of Remembrance, you're able to go to the "point of entry" to find out where your problem started. Yet this time there is no Council—it's just you and your guide, and sometimes a Master Teacher. You're then asked about what addiction or behavior you felt affected your life. The key word here is *affect:* When you're gambling, drinking, taking drugs, overspending, crippled by low self-esteem, dealing with a violent temper, or suffering from anything else that's taken over your mind, this negatively affects your life. Consequently, this is an overlay that you have to "baptize" away. (While baptism was originally started for "original sin," it's used on the Other Side to get rid of past-life traumas, carryovers, or any other negativity brought in by incoming souls.)

The Hall of Remembrance contains yet another type of scanning machine, but this one is in the round. It reminds me of an exhibit that Disneyland used to have years ago called "America the Beautiful," in which films were projected a full 360 degrees around you. You were literally surrounded by fields, streams, waterfalls, and mountains, along with stereophonic sound—your senses were so assailed that you felt you were really there in the middle of all the scenery. That's the way this scanner operates: It takes you to the very point that you had your first drink, smoked your first cigarette, or took your first drug; or to the initial circumstance that created your poor self-esteem or triggered the negative behavior that has kept you from attaining happiness or growth.

You may wonder why we have to scan again when we've already done so in other halls. Well, this particular scanner is specific to what caused the offending problem—it's a pictorial therapy session, if you will. Now it's not a cure-all for every single occurrence in life; rather, it has to do with the individual and what has crippled him or her mentally, morally, or physically. After all, many people can go through the same circumstances and have very different experiences. Maybe those with certain problems or carryovers have had an episode (point of entry) that was so dramatic that it really altered their whole view of themselves, which made life quite difficult. Yes, everyone has their charts (which they wrote for themselves), but the whole purpose of coming down to this planet is to learn to understand *and* overcome their lessons.

From what I've seen, it's not just one episode that shapes us; instead, that one thing is usually compounded by another (or others) from a past life. It's almost as if our inner God center or "soul mind" is trying to ask, "Are you ever going to get it?" We should never feel stupid if we don't. We all take a long time to learn . . . yours truly included. Francine told me when I was very young that coming into life, and especially the earthly shell, makes us dull and seemingly stupid; however, most of that is due to the loss of our subconscious memories.

As I get older, I realize how right she was, especially where the loss of memory is concerned—because if we did remember the Other Side, we'd probably never stay here. We'd all jump off the bridge, which wouldn't work because we'd just have to come right back to this hell of a planet all over again.

After Francine told our salon about the Hall of Remembrance, I again heard from many of the attendees. One man informed me that he'd tried everything to break his smoking habit, including pills, hypnosis, and the nicotine patch. Then one night he found himself in the hall with his male guide and a Master Teacher, and he watched himself in this life being surrounded by smokers. As a child, he'd even put a pencil in his mouth to simulate a cigarette;

or he'd get little scraps of white paper, glue them into tubes, and act as if he were smoking. Then his family bought him candy cigarettes—everyone laughed and thought it was so cute, and they all remarked how grown up he looked. Of course this was a definite point of entry, since he was being praised and encouraged for being so "cool."

Then the scene changed and he found himself in England. He was a wealthy, heavyset businessman who owned a lot of property, including a tobacco shop. He smoked big cigars constantly, not only to promote his business, but also because he felt it made him look important and prosperous. He died of pneumonia in that life, which was probably exacerbated by his smoking.

When my client woke up, he was surprised that he didn't want a cigarette—right then and there he felt that the problem had been resolved. Even though at times he still got a craving, it was so slight that it went away immediately. He'd gotten to the root of this weed in the garden of his life; by pulling it out, his need to associate himself with smoking was removed and his addiction ended.

So many times we begin to identify ourselves with our pains, phobias, or addictions; and this gets in the way of our growth and happiness and also squelches our spirituality. To that end, another woman told me about her problem with drinking, which she'd had for years—she'd been to rehab, gone through an intervention, and tried everything else she could think of to quit. After our salon, she went home and decided to try to reach the Hall of Remembrance through meditation. She was successful and was met by her female guide, along with two Master Teachers. She was also aware of two angels who were with her, which told me that she needed extra comfort and help.

This woman saw herself as a gal named Lil in the Wild West. She didn't seem to have a father around, and her mother was a prostitute at a local saloon and apparently always drunk. She picked up her mother's bottle one day and drank—the liquor made things appear brighter; and Lil didn't feel so poor, lonely, and despondent. And that's how addiction lures us into a false sense of euphoria or forgetfulness for a time. Yet the end result is always the same: Sooner or later, we end up paying the piper. We can never dull the edge on this life for long . . . we have to face it full-on at some point.

Anyway, Lil got older, started her own saloon, and was praised by the cowboys and farmers for how much she could hold her liquor. In her small, boring world, this was the only accomplishment she felt she could be proud of. And in those days, just like with smoking, people weren't educated to really understand what they were doing with, or to, their bodies, so Lil unfortunately died of pancreatic cancer.

My client had almost replicated that life in this one: She had an absentee father, and her mother was drunk most of the time. She also started to drink to get away from the hopeless feeling of being trapped, and she eventually got married and had a daughter. Her daughter was still very young, but this woman began to fear that she'd follow in the family footsteps. In addition, her husband, who had been so patient with her, was sadly coming to the realization that he didn't want to put up with this anymore.

Happily, she recently let me know that for seven months she hasn't had a single drink. She said it was enough to see how she'd wasted her life and had died such a painful death as Lil, but even more important, what she'd been doing to her daughter and husband had been a wake-up call. Her life had gotten so much better, and I know it will continue to do so.

Finally, I heard from another attendee who was not by any means morbidly obese but was much too heavy for her size. Her weight was affecting her back and knees, and she'd been diagnosed with diabetes. Yet even though she'd tried exercise, diets, starving herself, and having her thyroid checked, nothing made a difference.

She finally decided to ask God to let her go to the Hall of Remembrance during sleep to help her with this problem. She was met by a male guide, a Master Teacher, and two angels who seemed to stand at the temple's entrance. As she went in, she told me that the panoramic scene that began to revolve around her was so real that she felt she was almost there. Then she said something so very interesting, which I thought was incredibly descriptive:

"Everything came back to me like a long-dead or forgotten memory, and it came back with a great *swoosh*."

She first found herself as the "fat lady" in a freak show (although I've always hated that moniker). She'd grown up in Oklahoma, and a long drought had caused her poverty-stricken family to give her away to a traveling carnival that had come to town. This woman's sense of rejection and abandonment was so overwhelming that taking in more food was a way to fill the gaping hole that the lack of loved ones had left. The carnival owners encouraged her to eat—especially anything that was sweet, starchy, or fatty—because, of course, they made money off of people oohing and aahing at her huge girth.

Strangely, my client had felt a weird sense of acceptance because at least people were coming to see her and marveling at her weight. (Sometimes any attention, even if it's negative, is better than none at all.) She had her other "outcast" friends such as the midgets, the "lizard man," the sword swallowers, the Siamese twins, and so on; and they clung together and accepted each other. But this woman still felt trapped and alone in this body that sequestered the real person hiding inside. In that life, she died of a massive heart attack at the age of 30.

My client next saw herself in a desert, living the life of what she referred to as a type of bedouin (a nomadic desert dweller). There was never enough to eat in such an environment, as you can imagine, but the clan was smart enough to know where the different oases were; so they ate dates, berries, and various plants; and killed one of their goats every now and again. The group also traded with other tribes for money, or staples such as salt.

This woman was married with two boys, and her husband was a very cruel man who beat her often, sometimes for no reason. He had a brother who was the exact opposite—and the brother and the wife fell in love. I don't know where you feel you can hide in a desert, but I guess passion or lust wins out. Anyway, her husband was supposed to be on a scouting trip for the next oasis, but he'd come back early and discovered them making love behind a large rock. He immediately killed his brother by cutting his throat with a saber, yet instead of stoning his wife, he bound her hands and forced her to walk alongside the tribe as they traveled. They made her follow behind them on foot all day and refused to give her food or water. Then early the next morning her clan left her alone in the middle of the desert without provisions.

Since the women of that time always depended on men to find their way, they didn't know east from west or where the next resting place was; thus, this poor woman wandered for what seemed like days in the burning heat. She began to have delusions from sunstroke, and was so hungry and thirsty that she began to eat sand. She choked to death and mercifully died.

This story does have a satisfying ending, though. My client realized that she ate so much because she'd felt rejected and unaccepted in both lives. In addition, she now had a solution for another problem that had been plaguing her for many years: a scratchy sensation in her throat that no doctor had ever been able to diagnose. After seeing herself as a fat lady in the carnival and then witnessing the depression and shame she felt in her bedouin life that led to her subsequent death by eating sand, she lost weight very quickly and her throat returned to normal. So she got a two-for-one release, or as I prefer to call it . . . a blessing.

With all these temples available for your use, it can be really exciting to have the opportunity to visit them, get healings, and rid yourself of phobias and problems. In fact, before you even go into the meditative state to visit this hall, it's a good idea to make a list of the things you want to eliminate or be done with. It will make your session that much more effective. (If you'd indeed like to reach this temple through meditation, please turn to page 199 after reading the instructions on pages 181–184.)

Chapter 7

THE TEMPLE OF
GOD'S MESSENGERS

Even though the Temple of God's Messengers is Romanesque in design, it has a golden dome on top and looks more like a cathedral. Every type of religious symbol is also represented in its beautiful stained-glass windows—the cross, ankh, Star of David, star and crescent moon, bindu, yin and yang, symbol of Allah—you name it.

As you can guess from its name, the purpose of this temple is to give anyone the opportunity to talk to the great messengers, messiahs, and holy men and women of creation. When you come inside, the entities are aware of whom you came to see, and the one you need comes from behind a golden veil to meet you.

For instance, if you go in and ask for Jesus, he knows you want to see him and is instantly available to you. Naturally he can bilocate (as all can on the Other Side), being anywhere at once in his full essence; like all very advanced souls, he can be in countless places at once. Christ will embrace you and walk with you around this beautiful golden building that's filled with marble accents. And you can ask him any question at all, for it will always be answered.

The Other Side's magnificent rose garden is very near this temple, and many times you'll see entities walking with Jesus or some other great messenger there. This brings up a story that Francine once told my ministers concerning how I came to live this life. My spirit guide said that I was basically through with incarnating after doing so some 48 times, until Jesus cornered me one day and asked me to come with him through the rose garden. It was he and he alone who convinced me to come into this existence, which he said would be my last. Yet the planning for this life was so long that I had to go through five other incarnations first as part of my preparation. Hence, out of that one seemingly casual stroll with Jesus, I ended up with 54 lives instead of 48! I think that when I go back Home, he and I are going to have a little talk. . . .

Jesus will usually give you his hallowed blessing, along with insight into how he has been so misinterpreted by human beings, who have greatly strayed from the message he tried to get across. He doesn't have much respect for churches that put words in his mouth and then enact their political and moneymaking agendas—not to mention various dogmas—in his name. In fact, it seems that all of God's messengers feel the same way about this. (Francine says that I've spoken to Buddha, Mohammed, Apollonius of Tyana, and Zoroaster; as well as many other Divine mentors who are not in the hierarchy of direct messengers but are great rabbis, priests, clerics, and holy men and women in their own right.)

Behind every war, disruption, or chaotic event on this planet, you'll find religion. The dictionary defines *religion* as: "Belief in a personal God or gods entitled to obedience and worship." It can also be described as a "particular system" of worship, which is basically what is practiced on Earth. All major faiths feel they're the ones who are totally in the right—and while they all have *some* truth in them, none of them have *all* of the truth.

On the Other Side, where there is no dissension or negativity of any kind, you can then logically conclude that there is no religious discord either. In fact, there's not even religious dogma of any kind because there's no need for it. After all, when we pass over, our minds open up to full capacity, and the truth that has always existed in our subconsciousness comes to full awareness. We immediately note the strong and loving presence of our Creators, Who only cherish and adore us—and we become instantly cognizant of the fact that we love Them in return. For those of us who have never truly felt the love of God on Earth (which can never compare to how we feel on the Other Side), it can be quite a shock. This only lasts for a moment, however, because then we become acutely aware that this is Home, the true reality.

Think about it . . . why would religion ever be necessary here? There's no negativity, no evil, and nothing to be afraid of—so with everything being positive and good, nobody harms anyone else, and there's no need for rules or regulations (dogma). We're constantly filled with Mother and Father God's love and have no desire to disobey or cause any harm; instead, we just want to adore Them and live the wonderfully exciting and peaceful eternal existence that They have given us.

There are churches, synagogues, mosques, and many types of shrines on the Other Side for those who want to worship our Creators or pray to Them. However, no earthly religious ceremonies or traditions are followed or enacted—there aren't any masses, callings to prayer, readings of the Torah, evangelistic prayer meetings, or other products of Earth's environment because they're not needed. The places of worship exist for those who feel more comfortable in those surroundings for their own individual prayers, but religious ceremonies only take place on the holy days that are recognized on the Other Side, and they're more like joyful parties than anything else.

The Temple of God's Messengers is also visited by many who are going through orientation on the Other Side for the purpose of clarifying their earthly religious beliefs. It's especially beneficial for those whose practices bordered on being (or were) fanatical in nature, since these people can talk to their revered icons and get the truth right from the horse's mouth. So followers of evangelism can discover that God is not to be feared, and suicide bombers can learn that jihad or holy war is not wanted by God. It can be very difficult for some hard-core believers to find out that the religion they followed was wrong, but no one can deny the truth after talking to Jesus, Mohammed, Buddha, or any other religious figure whom they followed.

Now if you happen to stop by this hall without needing to see anyone, it wouldn't be unusual for you to catch the many messengers and holy men and women gathered together in theological discussion. Francine says that there's no disappointment as such from these entities, but there does seem to be this ongoing commentary on how human beings can create such havoc, wars, and bloodshed in their names. All of these truly holy and spiritual individuals tried to bring peace, love, and news of an all-loving God to humankind—who responded by tainting those teachings with its own political agendas and interpretations based on ego.

The Other Side is where you can find the authentic writings of the Koran, the Egyptian Book of the Dead, the Talmud, the *whole* Bible, and so many other lost writings from all of God's messengers—not the edited versions now used on Earth. You can read these original texts, along with the actual words the messiahs and messengers wrote or said. Francine says that everyone who does so is either surprised or horrified to discover that the dogma they were exposed to for so many years wasn't exactly the truth. What they thought were the genuine words and actions of these wonderful messengers were found to be highly suspect because humans changed and misinterpreted them so much for their own agendas.

Any real Bible student knows its real history and how the early Christians edited it, changed it, and had books thrown out while others were put in . . . such are the follies of humankind. It's not like today, when all speeches are recorded word for word. In ancient times, everything was either taken down by scribes or delivered by word of mouth to someone who could then put his own spin on it. That's one of the reasons why I write my books in longhand and have them typed from my original spiral notebooks, and even then I look everything over to make sure that they're indeed *my* words on the page. After I'm gone, no one will ever be able to say that I didn't write my own books. (Besides, there's something very personal about putting pen to paper . . . I feel like I'm writing a letter to all of my readers.)

Then when writings are translated into different languages, they sometimes lose their meaning because some words just don't translate—this is especially true with the Arabic and Aramaic languages, which just happen to be what the Koran and some parts of the Bible were originally written in. For example, when my book *Life on the Other Side* was translated into German, the title became *The Spirit World Is Not Closed.* You may say, "Well, that's not a big deal," but it kind of is, since it intimates that the spirit world (the Other Side) was closed at one time. This then raises unnecessary questions such as, "Wasn't it always open?" or "What do you mean—now it's opened up, but before it was shut?" I'm not being critical, but if this can happen with my own material, what do you think has happened for thousands of years with respect to other works?

Nevertheless, it's so wonderful to know that all of these messengers and direct reporters sent from God are available to each and every one of us when religions have made them so unapproachable. The Temple of God's Messengers is truly a blessed place to visit (and if you'd like to do so through meditation, please turn to page 201 after reading the instructions on pages 181–184).

Chapter 8

THE HALL OF
MEDITATION

This medium-sized temple has a long, rectangular shape, along with many columns supporting it both outside and in. It's extremely peaceful inside, with soft blue light that seems to emanate from the interior columns permeating throughout. There's a larger open space in the middle of the hall, but along the sides are small enclosed cubicles where people can go and tune in to heavenly music or just be alone and contemplate God's love and all the wonders and joys that abound in creation. Each cubicle has a window, through which one can hear the waterfall outside, or it can be kept closed for absolute silence.

After many people pass over, meet their loved ones, and visit the other temples that orient them to the Other Side, they find it comforting to go into the Hall of Meditation for prayer and to rejuvenate their minds. Lots of them will bring their programming from life with them, such as the need to use rosaries, prayer cards, worry beads, and the like. Some will kneel, and others will pray and bow to the east with their foreheads to the floor. This is all more than acceptable, but as time goes by, such habits will essentially drop away.

Yet this temple isn't just for orientation back to the Other Side. Even those who have been over there for eternity still visit to give honor to our Creators, which isn't much different from paying homage to God in this life. Everyone visits most of the temples many times, so they can gain a greater understanding or be of greater help to others, or even to garner a greater sense of peace and consciousness for their own souls. Please remember that we never stop growing or learning, even when we're on the Other Side.

Residents also come into the Hall of Meditation to send what they refer to as "prayer thoughts" to their incarnated loved ones, or to direct positive energy to Earth to help alleviate its tribulations, famines, wars, and so forth. This makes me feel really good, for as a girl in Catholic school, I was told to "pray for the dead," and masses were always said for the deceased. I used to wonder why we were praying for them—they were in a perfect environment with God, without all the sickness and evil that this world holds. We were the ones in hell, so why didn't *they* pray for *us?* So it not only made sense but was a great comfort to me to discover that those beyond the veil *are* sending energy, hope, and love to us to help us get through this life.

Now while we always think of meditation as quiet, the center of the Hall of Meditation is filled with a beautiful cadence of harmonious chants. Whether it's "om," "sa tu na ma," "shalom," or "kyrie eleison," it all seems to blend. Keep in mind that these ancient sounds have been infused in humankind and have been used in its religions, but any noise or name that's pleasing or that quiets and opens up the mind is fine. That's why transcendental meditation (TM) works so well for some people.

So if you try chanting with your meditation, do be sure that the word(s) you choose and your visualization are special to you on an emotional level, for you'll find that your meditation is much more effective. For example, I love to take a deep breath, hold it for ten seconds, and then exhale while doing my beloved chant of "Azna." I also find that when you chant during meditation it helps to think of a beautiful scene in nature, such as a stream, mountain, or ocean. I personally like to envision fields of golden daffodils (gold is Azna's color).

Francine agrees with me that it's impossible to just have a "blank mind" because we're active, thinking spirits with a soul mind that works on many levels. We'd almost have to have a lobotomy to be completely blank, and even then I'm not too sure that there wouldn't be *some* brain activity. Even if the physical brain at death shows nothing on the monitor, the essence of our soul mind is still active—we've just left our old, faulty physical bodies behind.

Also, keep in mind that almost no one has time for three or four hours of meditation. It's not that I'm being judgmental if you feel like having an existence composed of so much reflection, but unless you're up on a mountaintop or locked away in a cell, I doubt that you'll be able to have any kind of a life. After all, while Jesus himself prayed and meditated, nowhere does it say that he spent hours at a time sequestered away and doing so (except for his time in the desert).

I'm good friends with a dear, saintly Carmelite nun who lives in a cloistered convent; and she's told me that they pray, have mass, and meditate in the evening for all the souls in the world—but then they also visit with family members, garden, cook, clean, and telephone friends. (Yes, she has special times when she can call me or when I can call her, but our calls are never limited.) She's also taking a trip to Europe and even going to visit the Holy Father, whom she grew up with. So even nuns are too active to spend all day kneeling in prayer and meditation.

Of course there are some members of religious sects such as Opus Dei who *do* spend hours in prayer, meditation, and corporal mortification . . . the last of which I don't understand. If Jesus said that our bodies are our temples, why would we deface, maim, or hurt them? Francine agrees that Jesus never wanted us to hurt ourselves to show our love for him, but rather to do good works in his name. Like all of God's messengers, he tried to lift up human-kind with the hope of a better place and a better way to live. From Christ's simple statements and parables (which were never rules), we humans have managed to form occult groups, controlling reli-gions, and dogmas all in the name of "God."

Again and again I've said to do what feels good, right, just, and logical to *you*. If it doesn't, you should stop, for this is truly your inner God center telling you that something you're doing isn't for you.

Yesterday, for instance, I read for a woman who'd been bound in this strict, meditative, constantly praying group for 30 years, and she said, "Thank you, Sylvia. Your books—which I wasn't supposed to read—set me free."

I replied, "You're welcome . . . and I'm not being humble, but your soul was ready to listen. So give *yourself* a big pat on the back."

After Francine presented information on the Temple of Meditation in the infamous salon, we received several letters and e-mails reporting that people were able to go to this hall and that their subsequent meditations were much more successful than normal. Many of them had also used our Gnostic chant "Arem, Shem, Beth Sedal, Sacravalian, Ahad," which means "Blessed be this Queen on high, Who is sacred to all that come to Her."

Francine gave me this chant many years ago, and when I asked her what language it was in, she said, "None that is known now." Apparently it's an archaic combination of words or sounds that describe and give homage to the Mother God, and they go so far back into antiquity that researchers on the Other Side have charted them to be thousands of years old and have determined that they came through an early prophet. My study groups and churches use this chant all the time and report that they reap tremendous benefits from it.

One woman who attended the salon lost all traces of the depression that she'd suffered from for 20 years, a man who was bipolar and still on medication (which you should never stop without first consulting your physician) now felt in control and more like himself than he had since he was in his teens, and a woman who had lost her son and was in such indescribable grief felt a great lifting of her spirits.

However, it's important to understand that while the Hall of Meditation can inspire healing, it's primarily meant for prayer, honor, adoration, and gratitude . . . as well as for helping others. Although the Other Side doesn't have religions per se because our minds are so open over there that we know the real truths and continually feel the energy and love of our Creators, this temple is nevertheless a place where everyone gives homage to Them.

As I mentioned before, many beyond the veil use the Hall of Meditation to send prayers and energy to those in life. (Francine says that she often sees my father there sending me energy and help.) And angels are always in attendance, as they are everywhere. My spirit guide calls them the "lightning bolt" messengers: As soon as a meditative thought of goodwill, hope, or positive energy is created, the angels carry it in a blink of an eye to the person it's meant for.

Have you ever been in dire straits and then gotten this overwhelming feeling that *everything will be all right?* Well, that would be a case where the angels are delivering their message to you. Unfortunately, thanks to this negative environment and all its programming, your so-called intelligence or overly stressed emotions probably got in and negated the positive, causing you to fall right back into the "what-ifs."

Anyway, it's enough to spend just ten or even five minutes a day in meditation, and the best time to practice is early in the morning. It won't hurt you one bit to set your alarm ten minutes early—it may be difficult the first few mornings, but soon you'll find that your days are going so much better. To take those extra minutes and simply chant or put your mind in a beautiful place can make a big difference. (Do make sure that you also envision the white light of the Holy Spirit around you every morning; and ask that this day sees you doing good and being a true, living example of God.) Once you get used to this wonderful spiritual ritual, whether it be as an individual or in a group, you'll want to continue doing it, because the benefits are immeasurable.

Then if you're not too tired in the evenings, take some time before you go to bed to breathe in love and positive thoughts and exhale negativity. It's a type of shower to cleanse you of whatever you've absorbed throughout the day, which your conscious memory may not even be aware of. I do all of the above, as well as praying to keep my loved ones safe and to do my best in all situations. Then I chant for a few minutes—I realize that God knows what I want, so I don't have to exhaust myself or feel guilty about not doing enough.

I'm always amazed when people don't understand that God knows their hearts, minds, souls, charts, and what they came down here for. It's like they feel that He won't pay attention unless they "storm the heavens." Even with my church's prayer groups, we just ask that you give us your name, and we'll ask for God's healing grace. We don't need to know your malady because He already does.

(If you'd like to reach this temple through meditation, please turn to page 205 after reading the instructions on pages 181–184.)

※ ※ ※

Chapter 9

THE TEMPLE OF RETREAT (THE TOWERS)

While the Towers are not temples as such, their function is very important, so I decided to include them in this book.

What those on the Other Side simply refer to as "the Retreat" are two large twin buildings that are primarily constructed of dark blue glass. The Towers are set a little bit behind the other halls, and each of them is about 60 stories high and has many rooms. The rooms themselves are comfortable but fairly sparse, containing a downy-soft recliner, lots of books, and a chair that's next to a table laden with paper and writing implements. The only adornments are vases full of fresh, lush flowers, which give off a wonderful potpourri of scent that seems to fill each room.

There aren't any beds or restrooms because, although we have internal organs on the Other Side, we don't need to sleep or go to the bathroom. Sometimes when we first come over we bring with us leftovers or cravings from life on Earth, so we want a drink or a smoke or something to eat. This soon diminishes, though, and we no longer desire those things. Similarly, there is no need for electricity (which is only used in experimental and creative temples and centers) because it's like dawn or twilight all the time . . . a lovely and soft pinkish or rose-tinged light is continually diffused throughout the Other Side, so there is no distinction between day and night.

Almost all incoming souls are either sent to the Towers or go there of their own accord. This is not a place for those who need counseling over traumas experienced on Earth, but is rather a private area for reflection or prayer. Those who come here enjoy great serenity, as they look out over meadows, lakes, streams, and mountains; see wildlife in great abundance; and listen to beautiful, heavenly music. They may choose to go out and walk the paths that are prevalent throughout the grounds; or they might prefer to write, relax with a good book, meditate, pray, or just sit and contemplate. And Francine says that two people rarely share the same room, not even members of the same family, as this is a place to regroup. The Towers do have attendants (facilitators) on call for any need such as aromatherapy or to conduct yoga or tai chi sessions.

From what Francine has told me, this wonderful retreat of bliss and tranquility reminds me of my time at St. Teresa College in Kansas City, Missouri. I'd see the priests and nuns strolling our campus at twilight reading their missals, while I'd go down the lush hill and sit at the grotto of Mary (whom I knew to be Azna). It was so peaceful, with birds overhead and the sound of cicadas in the early-evening hours, that I can truly understand the serenity my guide describes . . . or at least as close as I'll get to it in this life.

The Temple of Retreat is such a popular place on the Other Side because all of us have a closer and stronger rapport with Mother and Father God there; and with our minds opened up to their full capacity, we often seek reflection and intimacy with Them on an individual basis. In fact, some cocooned entities are sent here after they emerge for that very reason, especially if they've gone through a particularly horrifying exit.

Speaking of exits from Earth, I'd like to make it clear here that I've never talked to any spirits who have had a painful death—either they're out of their body before it happens or they don't remember it at all. Anything that those of us who are left behind see is only the neurological and autonomous nervous system reacting or activating; the soul itself is already gone.

In the case of entities who have experienced rapid or horrendous exits, however, their souls may become confused or traumatized, so cocooning, sleep, and being at the Towers can help to assimilate and orientate them back to the Other Side. They're not in any physical pain—nor are they lonely, regretful, or missing life on Earth. Sometimes such souls just need a little TLC. It's like when I return from an exhausting trip and my personal assistant, Linda, says, "Why don't you take a nice hot bath, get your robe on, lie down, and rest. I'll fix you some tea and unpack for you." It's just a warm and loving transition back Home.

Right after the salon with Francine, I received a call from an attendee who wanted to know if I knew about these "new" buildings she'd discovered on the Other Side. She'd meditated and visited two of the temples that my guide had given information about and was delighted about that, but she wanted me to know that she'd also seen two tall buildings covered entirely in blue glass! Now Francine hadn't mentioned the Towers in this particular trance, and evidently this woman hadn't read my earlier books in which I've mentioned them, as she was so excited and gushed out this information before I could get a word in. She said, "I went in and felt such peace, and a coming together of my mind."

It seems that before this meditation, she'd been on every kind of medication available for anxiety—and now, with her doctor's help, she was ready to go off all of it. She'd been healed of her long struggle by going into these so-called new buildings, and she was very eager to share her "discovery" with me so that it might help others.

I have to admit here that moments like this are part of why I keep doing what I do, regardless of the fact that I already knew about the Towers. This woman had validated their existence because she didn't know of them before; what's even more important is that she wanted to share what she'd discovered in order to help others. I'm not saying that I don't get tired sometimes, but the passing on of valid information (which comes from God, not me) and the assistance it gives people is what brings me the joy and the drive to carry on. Like my client, I also try to use what I've been given; if I didn't, I don't think I would have lasted for more than five decades in the business. After all, we can have all the intention in the world, but passion and love are what ultimately drive us all.

(If you'd like to reach the Towers through meditation, please turn to page 209 after reading the instructions on pages 181–184.)

PART II

Different Temples for Different Levels

Chapter 10

THE TEMPLE
OF LEVELS

As I've explained in some of my prior books, there are levels on the Other Side that are classified as such mainly for purposes of vocation and organization. Now a person on the third level (which involves working with plants and animals) isn't less evolved than a person on the sixth (which holds teachers and orientators). Francine says that most entities move freely through all the levels, and souls may find themselves working in the scientific field (fifth level) for their main job yet also love to garden (third level) and do that as well. She says that it varies with all individuals, but what souls do as their primary vocation at Home is directly related to their theme of perfection. And since everyone has a passion for their work over there, hobbies are of secondary importance.

There are temples that correspond with each level, although residents of the Other Side tend to go to all of them. Thanks to the meditations I've provided in Part IV, you'll also have the chance to visit these very interesting halls—the only exception is this first one, the Temple of Levels, which exists solely for those beyond the veil. However, I thought it was important to provide information about it so that you can understand more about its function and about the levels themselves.

While it's just a single-story building, this hall nevertheless takes up a lot of room. It looks more Egyptian in design, with short columns that are a glowing rust color and earth-toned exterior walls. It has numerous doors leading into it from all sides; and while it isn't as ornate as many of the other temples, it's still a very beautiful structure.

This is the site where everyone meets about once a week in our time, thus giving all entities the opportunity to explore what's happening on all the levels. Of course everyone on the Other Side sees and mingles with each other all the time, but this is different in that it's geared to fresh ideas and to the expansion of knowledge.

Usually what's discussed at these meetings in the Temple of Levels are new developments in the various fields of endeavor, and feedback is always welcome. For example, those working in animal husbandry may pass on information to other individuals involved in research to help make their experiments more efficient. Or artists and craftspersons may offer ideas to architects that they would then go on to incorporate into a new building design.

Francine told me that she once happened upon some orientators talking to a Council member about more innovative ways to assist outgoing souls to Earth. (As an aside, it's far more traumatic to be born than to experience death and go Home.) She said that the group then reminded the outgoing souls in attendance what they'd be learning and how short the experience would be—I guess you might call it a "pep talk." Naturally, encouraging speeches are given to all souls, but they're always fine-tuning things on the Other Side.

My spirit guide also overheard some researchers talking about improving transplants; and then they discussed the benefits of stem-cell research and how it should be employed, especially for neurological concerns and problems with the pancreas, lungs, and liver. She said they agree that we on Earth can use umbilical cords instead of embryos to get stem cells, for it's just as effective, and they were even studying the placenta as a way to cure illness.

Apparently these researchers were also very upset about what they called "synthetic medicines" coming out for the benefit of pharmaceutical companies and were adamantly against the use of rats, mice, and other animals in research experiments—and not just because they're living things; rather, they felt the molecular and genetic structures were wrong, so experiments utilizing them wouldn't be that helpful. These researchers were more in favor of using volunteers from death row, or even those who had terminal illnesses and thus no hope of life. But they especially stressed that if the people they were trying to infuse with knowledge just let the information come through—without money, ego, or politics rearing their heads—the remedies for diseases would manifest rapidly, without anyone having to sacrifice lives or bodies.

Francine says that the Other Side has been trying to get a cure infused for AIDS and HIV that strangely uses a vaccination derived from the green monkey that lives mainly in Africa. (I don't understand the specifics, so I'm just reporting what she told me.) Yet they *have* found cures for cancer and other illnesses, but even when the information is infused, many on Earth don't pay attention—after all, if you create a remedy, there's no more money to gain from all the treatments. This is so sad, yet I've always felt that it was true. The medical industry is much like the food business in that it knows what's healthy, yet it keeps putting out junk for profit. So if a pharmaceutical company discovers a cure for an illness, it can then cut out many of the products that it manufactures for treatment of that same illness. It's a double-edged sword, not to mention a serious conflict of interest.

I think it's terrible that so many of my clients have to go to other countries such as Germany, Switzerland, and Sweden to procure drugs and procedures not approved in the United States. Now when it comes to plastic surgery, I find that going out of the country can be risky, especially if the motivation is to save money. We don't always know (and often can't check) the background or education of foreign doctors, and the medical standards in developing nations are usually below those of Europe or the United States.

Speaking of plastic surgery, I was surprised to hear from Francine that most researchers on the Other Side don't approve of invasive liposuction; in fact, she said there will be a new technique that utilizes electric currents, which will be a highly effective and noninvasive way to "battle the bulge." She also said that they were not at all excited about laparoscopic surgery for the stomach because there will be a safe hormone injection that will take weight off in the near future.

My spirit guide says that two of the most frequent subjects talked about in the Temple of Levels are global warming and the possibility of an asteroid crashing into our planet. Earth is experiencing record temperatures, the glaciers are melting rapidly, and we have holes in our ozone layer. Hurricanes are appearing in greater numbers and are seriously affecting parts of the United States. The world outside of the U.S. will see more tsunamis, earthquakes, and volcanic activity; as well as stronger typhoons and increased flooding. According to Francine, the researchers have said that they can still hold off devastation for many years and that the world will survive, but sooner or later humankind will destroy the ecological balance to the point where we'll all just go back Home.

Francine states that what we're currently experiencing on Earth has happened to almost all planets. Most worlds have had a volcanic age, an ice age, and then a warming trend; and many of them have then swung out of their orbits to be replaced by other planets and orbits that can sustain life. It's also interesting to note that according to my guide, not only do individuals have charts, but so do planets, as well as different countries, states, and territories. She explains that she can't find any records that indicate that we on Earth will begin to reincarnate on any other planet in this solar system after life here ends, but many humans have already incarnated elsewhere throughout the universe. She assures me that most of us won't incarnate again after our world eventually ends but will instead stay on the Other Side and keep learning for God.

While those beyond the veil know that global warming will take many years to get to a danger point, they feel that it's gone too far and are therefore concentrating on lessening its effects. And they believe that the impact from any significant asteroid is also years away, although they do know that the dinosaurs were killed off from such an impact earlier in Earth's history.

The discussions go on and on . . . and even though they know that we all have our charts to work out, getting through the negativity and infusing needed information are the hardest of tasks because those on this plane often don't listen. It's like when you're going on a trip and the travel agent, hotel personnel, and activity directors all try to make it the best one possible. Not long ago, for instance, I was in New York doing *Montel,* and they put me up in one of the fanciest hotels in the city. This is an establishment that has an excellent reputation around the world, yet the alarm system was broken and went off at all hours, the toilet wouldn't flush (my favorite), and one phone in the room was dead. Of course the people in the hotel helped make a bad situation better by taking the night off Montel's bill and moving us to another room. So it is with the Other Side, as they're constantly trying to help us down here in hell.

This experience made me think that I need to be more specific in my prayers to Azna before I travel, perhaps saying something along the lines of "Please let the trip go smoothly, without any disastrous incidents. I can learn patience, but not to the point that I'm tearing my hair out." After all, you can't change your chart, but you *can* modify it and ask for miracles, both of which are our Mother's specialties.

Miracles can also happen because of the "option line," which is the one area of your chart that's left open. So I tell my clients that instead of feeling like victims of their charts, they should be happy because they get this one area that they can write in as they go. For example, my option line is family, so rather than being a victim of my mother, as my sister was, I chose to align myself with my father and grandmother, and later on I continually used affirmations about my children and grandchildren. Thank God I did all this, because I didn't have sons who went to jail or got into gangs, drugs, or what have you. Are they angels? No, but my God, they're both wonderful fathers, even though they really never had one . . . just me. But through my teaching them, along with the makeup of their own beautiful souls, they became great parents.

My boys were lucky enough to have father figures such as my dear dad, as well as a neighbor across the street named Dewey. In fact, Dewey took my oldest son, Paul, under his wing—and the sad thing was that his own son didn't seem to care about him at all. Paul was even with Dewey when he died and helped talk him over to the Other Side.

In addition, both boys had Dr. Marvin Small in their lives, a saintly man who helped me through some frantic times in my life. He did it with the positive attitude that "Everything will be all right" and "Everything will be fixed," which you don't tend to hear anymore. When my youngest, Chris, got a terrible staph infection deep in his leg (he fell in the kitchen while cleaning and caught his shin on a step), it became so infected that it was as if he had some sort of leg-eating disease. They wouldn't touch him at an emergency clinic, although a doctor there did tell my son that he'd lose his leg. Well, of course I was out of my mind, so I called Dr. Small, who calmly assured me, "Sylvia, I promise you that I won't let this happen." He put Chris in the hospital, and while my son was so out of it that he couldn't understand why he saw five doctors in one day, he completely recovered and got to keep his leg.

Dr. Small was not only my boys' pediatrician, but he was a dear and cherished friend as well. His name was certainly a misnomer and a standing joke, as he was about 6'6" tall and was absolutely revered in the medical world. He didn't talk about his accomplishments that much because he was very genial and unassuming, but one night over dinner, his wife let slip that he was proud of the fact that not one of his patients had ever died. Naturally, this is unheard of in this day and age, so the conversation turned to how much medicine has advanced, as well as Small's prowess as a doctor.

As we all were singing his praises, you could tell he was getting embarrassed, and he quietly said, "No, it's not me who deserves the praise."

I replied, "Marvin, not to lose one patient in all your years of practice is amazing, and you deserve the credit."

He calmly answered, "No, I don't." He paused and went on, "Oh, sure, I'm trained and educated to heal as a doctor, but I made a pact with God many years ago when I first started practicing medicine that if He would do His part, I would do mine. He has never failed to do His part, and believe me, I've seen some miracles."

I knew this was very personal for him (his wife later confirmed this by telling me that he'd never spoken to anybody about his pact with God), but I had to ask one last question: "What do you do when you have a case where your patient is in danger of dying?"

He smiled a little sheepishly and merely said, "I pray for them. It has never failed. Now let's talk about something else."

I'm convinced that this wonderful man had a special rapport with God and an almost uncanny ability to heal his little patients. He loved children and would instantly make them laugh and feel at ease. When Paul shattered his elbow after falling off the monkey bars, doctors at the emergency room told me that he'd have to have pins inserted into his elbow and that one of his arms would be shorter than the other. Even though my son was a teenager at the time, I took him to see Dr. Small, who got Dr. Richard Mercer (an orthopedic surgeon and another dear friend) involved. After consulting with each other, they simply put a sling around my boy's neck and forearm and let the elbow hang free. This worried me, but I was assured by both of them that it would heal . . . and it did. Paul didn't have to have surgery, there weren't any pins, and that arm isn't shorter than the other.

Now you know why I think Dr. Small is a saint. As Francine says, there are some souls who are so advanced that they do indeed have a special rapport with our Creators and perform miracles, usually without anyone really knowing about it. I believe that this is the case with Dr. Small.

So when times are tough, please don't think that all is lost. It's just like my guide has always told me: "When you're down on this earthly plane and everything seems so hard to learn because it's accompanied by pain, loss, illness, and the like, you have to remember that it's all for the advancement of your soul." You can petition Azna, and always know that you have your option line, as well as saintly souls right here on Earth who can give you assistance. And remember that the entities beyond the veil are continually striving to improve things on this planet.

(Please note that since the Temple of Levels exists solely for residents of the Other Side, there's no need for a meditation to take you there.)

❦ ❦ ❦

Chapter 11

THE TEMPLE
OF LEARNING

According to Francine, while all the halls on the Other Side are always bustling, this one is by far the busiest. It seems that all the levels' residents come here at one time or another, and many even visit on what would be considered a "daily" basis in our time.

The Temple of Learning is very large and rectangular in shape, with exterior columns that are placed about every eight feet or so around the building, and it appears to emit a golden hue. Its architecture is Egyptian, with the colonnades featuring lotus decorations that are ringed in a dark brown, as well as a large obelisk outside the main entrance. The embossed wood doors have writings in many different languages on them, including hieroglyphics and cuneiform, symbolizing the various cultures of humankind. This hall is somewhat austere looking, with many small windows, but it's still quite beautiful.

You could almost say that the Temple of Learning is our Home's "great library," as it is a storehouse of the human race's written and oral knowledge. It contains every type of book, scroll, or whatever has been written on Earth, including a copy of the Rosetta stone in its complete form. But what's especially amazing is that it also houses similar works from the Other Side and other planets—Francine says that the writings in this temple are in every language from every country and every time, even those that no longer exist, such as ancient Sumeria, Babylonia, and Atlantis. Any language in the universe can be learned in no time when we're Home, which certainly helps when we're trying to understand long-lost communications in our constant mode of learning.

I've always been saddened by the burning of the Library of Alexandria because it held so much of Earth's history. There were extensive records about Atlantis, Lemuria, and other lost civilizations; as well as those of great historians, philosophers, and scientists . . . and it all went up in flames thanks to human stupidity. Imagine how excited I was when Francine said that copies of all of these documents are in the Temple of Learning in all their glory, and not one page is damaged.

There's so much information to be found in this hall, even with respect to what we consider the world's mysteries, from UFOs to the lost embalming techniques of the ancient Egyptians, which scientists still can't duplicate today. Works of Plato, Socrates, Aristotle, and other renowned philosophers are there, as are those of all the eminent historians from every culture and civilization. Ancient Sanskrit scrolls, Shakespeare's original plays, and the writings of Jesus all reside in this building. Just as the Louvre in Paris houses art from various sources, the Temple of Learning contains countless tomes from all cultures and civilizations.

Francine says that when entities come Home from a life and have finished their orientation, they're especially drawn to this temple and the Hall of Research (which I'll discuss in the next chapter) because they want to catch up on all the new discoveries and developments that have occurred since they incarnated. I think this shows how everyone on the Other Side is not only constantly interested in their own growth and learning, but they're all concerned with those of us still in life as well.

In fact, so many times when I'm stuck on a subject, my spirit guide will go to the Temple of Learning and check up on it for me. She's told me that there are millions of items we haven't even touched on, which makes my head hurt. Sure, I've gained a lot of information from all my years of readings and research, but the material on the Other Side is so vast that I always ask for her help.

She explains that the Temple of Learning is easier to access by subject rather than going through everything in the Hall of Records, and you'll see people talking to each other in different languages because of what they're researching, even though Aramaic is the common language of our Home.

There are thousands of facilitators or attendants to help you find what you're looking for in this hall. These attendants will point you to the area you're learning about or are interested in, and they'll also direct you to related topics that can augment your studies. If you do get stuck, there are all kinds of experts available to explain what you may be confused about. But mostly they just have vast knowledge as far as where to find information on any subject that has been written—and even more interesting, what hasn't been discovered on Earth yet. Again, this just goes to show that all of our past, present, and future knowledge is always kept safe for us on the Other Side.

After Francine presented information on the Temple of Learning at our salon, several attendees were kind enough to send me letters about their experiences when they went home and meditated on this hall. For example, one man wrote that he always wanted to know about the life of Benjamin Franklin, so he kept meditating on the Temple of Learning until one night he found himself there. He proceeded to describe the inside of this building in more detail than Francine had time for during the trance. He said that he knew he was in the right place because he was directed to the writings and biography of Mr. Franklin by a male facilitator who was dressed in what he said looked like "a green toga with a gold rope belt." My client remembered so much of this journey that he's decided to write a book about it.

I also received a note from a woman who said that she was somewhat in awe when she heard Francine describe this temple because her grandmother had told her that she'd gone to a place like this before, and had even authored a comprehensive volume about George Washington based on the information she'd gathered there. I'd actually read this book long before the salon, and there are so many interesting and unknown facts scattered throughout, such as our first President's beliefs in Freemasonry, what his temperament was like, his aggravation at supposedly chopping down that cherry tree, and many more little tidbits about his life.

I know that my books and those of so many other writers—especially those who pen works on famous figures previously unknown to them—are infused or are products of the Temple of Learning, whether they realize it or not. Such authors go over there, research their subjects, and bring their newfound knowledge back. *Ben Hur*, for instance, was written by General Lew Wallace, a Union general who served during the Civil War. He knew nothing about ancient Rome or Palestine, yet critics said that his novel was so accurate in its descriptions it was as if he'd actually lived there.

Wallace finished his manuscript in 1880 while he was governor of the New Mexico territory, and then later on he indeed visited Palestine. He was happy to see that what he'd described was so spot-on that he's quoted as saying he would not change one word of his book. The general also wrote two other novels that were historical in nature: *The Fair God,* about the conquest of the Aztecs by the Spanish; and *The Prince of India,* about the fall of Constantinople in 1453. Although General Wallace was undoubtedly influenced by his times in Mexico and Turkey, I believe that he also got a lot of his information about these three diverse cultures and distinctly different subjects from the Other Side.

I'm certain that much of the inspiration behind great artists, singers, musicians, and the like also comes in from past-life experiences. For example, Francine says that *Drums Along the Mohawk* was written by Walter D. Edmonds, who had a life as an Indian scout during the period he wrote about in that very book. The plots of many novels are cell memories from past existences, as are individual talents that people have, which doesn't take anything away from anyone's ability. The late English medium Rosemary Brown would channel Mozart and Bach, for instance, and come forth with brilliant compositions. Many virtuosos in the music field have validated these pieces, saying that they were in the same tempo or style in which the famous composers wrote. I don't know that much about music, but experts in the field certainly do, and Francine also said that Ms. Brown's work was indeed infused by the Other Side.

Similarly, Mary Shelley, the author of *Frankenstein*, stated that she just got up one night and was compelled to write the book, which simply flowed through her to paper. Also, look at Joseph Campbell—I cannot believe that as much as he read, he'd just sit around and let it rattle. Don't you think that he was often in an astral state in the Temple of Learning? My guide says that this is absolutely true, as no one on Earth can keep that much information in his or her mind.

When I was researching my book *The Mystical Life of Jesus,* I personally went to this hall for assistance (of course Francine helped me, too). And many times when I'm lecturing, I find myself putting forth things that I didn't think I knew, or that I *did* know and found out later were true. That's because the night before, I prayed, "Dear God, please infuse me with knowledge I don't have."

So, needless to say, if you choose to visit the Temple of Learning, you can get a comprehensive look at someone's life as they lived it and not just the contract they wrote. While the Hall of Records does have the "living" scanners, many individuals don't like being *in* a record of someone's life—they worry about the person's privacy, as well as the fact that they wouldn't want someone snooping around *their* lives. It seems as invasive as reading another person's private diary. However, Francine says that no one cares on the Other Side because they all feel that researching is part of the human experience and another tool that individuals can use in order to augment their souls. She says that people just look at these records as true biographies.

Now sometimes we do have an affinity for some character in history, not because we *were* this person, but because we might have known him or her in a previous life. Yet as I've said on *Montel,* out of the many readings and hypnosis regressions that I've done in more than 50 years as a practicing psychic, I've never found anyone who's lived a really notorious life. Maybe fame is relegated to a last life, but even then the odds of a person being renowned are very small because in comparison to all the existences lived, there are very few famous ones. I consider anyone who's made a large impact on history or humankind to be notable, so I don't include most actors (the majority of whom won't be remembered 100 years from now) or sports figures in that category. I'm not knocking the entertainment industry because many people do appreciate it, but *really* famous individuals have usually made a great worldwide impact in some way.

That doesn't mean that we all have to be in the limelight, because many who *are* have told me that it's very difficult, just as anyone's last life usually is. The rich and famous in our society—at least the many whom I've encountered—are more unhappy than you'd believe. It seems that because they're so well known, no one approaches them on a personal level or asks them out since their status is so intimidating, they spend a lot of time alone without any romance in their lives. Their main alternative is to date other celebrities because that's whom they interact with the most . . . and this is almost always a recipe for disaster.

It's quite difficult to be in love with a famous person because of the amount of attention he or she gets—it takes a very secure individual to deal with always being pushed in the background or to handle the lack of privacy that this person generates and has to fight daily. The reason most marriages between celebrities fail is also usually caused by ego: If one is more popular or has a more successful career, the self-image of the mate takes a hit because that person is generally used to being adored as well. (The movie *A Star Is Born* is a prime example of this scenario.) In addition, long separations can occur due to the very nature of their careers, and this certainly doesn't help.

What most people don't realize is that famous men and women have the same fears, anxieties, and insecurities that we all have . . . along with a few of their own, such as "Will people forget me?" "Am I getting too old?" "Who will take care of me when my career's over?" "Will I make enough money?" and so forth. Often, such individuals become hooked on drugs or alcohol and end up like Gloria Swanson's character in the movie *Sunset Boulevard.*

The very wealthy (and of course celebrities can fall into this category) have similar problems. They especially wonder if people love them for themselves or for their money and status, so they find themselves having to look for partners in high society or in richer families because of the fear of gold diggers. Prenuptial agreements run rampant, and they're not a good start to any relationship because they certainly don't indicate that trust is present.

I once had a professor who said, "You may think things are new or that it's something you haven't heard of, but there is nothing new under God's sun." I certainly don't ever claim to know one-millionth of all human behavior, but what I've learned in more than 70 years would fill tomes.

So if you're interested, definitely go to the Temple of Learning. Whether you're doing some research on a particular subject or person, have an interest in a new invention, or are curious about the latest advances in medicine . . . make sure you have a specific subject that you want to find out about, and bring your purpose with you when you visit this wonderful hall. (If you'd like to do so through meditation, please turn to page 211 after reading the instructions on pages 181–184.)

Chapter 12

THE HALL
OF RESEARCH

The next building we're going to examine looks like the Temple of Artemis that used to exist in Ephesus, which is in present-day Turkey. It was intended for the worship of (and sacrifices to) the Greek goddess of hunting, nature, and fertility. It was very famous in its time and was even one of the Seven Wonders of the World. From the pictures I've seen of what this temple used to look like, the Hall of Research is almost an exact replica, made of pink marble with blue streaks running through it, and seeming to emit a soft white light. While it appears somewhat Romanesque, it's definitely Grecian in design in that it has smaller columns—yet these are 60 feet tall and spaced so that there's plenty of room between them. There's also a large porch on the side of this hall, which is quite open and airy inside.

Again, the reason I want to describe these temples for you is so you understand that everything that's beautiful on our planet was in existence on the Other Side first. Think of ancient architecture: How could people with no real formal education even conceive of such sophisticated structures? Why wouldn't they just build functional square buildings instead? So many people think that human imagination or genius brings forth remarkable creations or inventions, but they actually come from the Other Side, where our minds operate at full capacity. They're then implanted into Earth's architects, builders, artists, and so forth.

The Hall of Research is where scientists, inventors, theologians, historians, artisans, writers, doctors, and a host of others do their exploration and experimentation. Every type of object, thought, or structure is made here; and the research goes on and on. You may ask, "Why would people have to do research if God already knows everything?" Well, we must do this in order to gain knowledge to magnify our souls for God, and He knows this. And it's an eternal thing, which comforts me. I mean, wouldn't it be terrible if we got to a point where we thought we knew it all? Thankfully, this will never happen. As Francine has told me, knowledge is infinite, and the more she finds out, the more she realizes she needs to learn.

Countless discoveries in every field of endeavor imaginable have originated in this very building. There's not one that's been made on Earth that didn't originate in the Hall of Research first, and there are millions more that have yet to be implanted or infused into humankind. Cures for myriad diseases and illnesses have been discovered on the Other Side, and many have already been given to various scientists on our planet. Bureaucracy and time-consuming experiments have prevented these cures from having an immediate impact, but they are indeed forthcoming. My guide says that because Earth is a school for the soul to learn in, there will always be incurable diseases as part of its environment. We can see this readily in the many reports of how disease mutates into different forms that become impervious to known cures. It seems that as fast as we find a way to remedy one disease, another one pops up.

Francine says that she's joined in and worked on some medical research herself, and she feels there will be breakthroughs in the treatment of cancer, diabetes, and immune-deficiency illnesses within the next few years. The cure for AIDS has been infused, and it's just a matter of time before it manifests. In addition, they're working on amazing electronics. I'm reminded of when my spirit guide told me years ago that there would be cars that wouldn't run on gasoline, and I just put it on the back burner of my mind—but now it's becoming commonplace to see hybrids and electric vehicles on the road.

Keep in mind that there are two main ways that information from the Other Side gets to the Earth plane: (1) carried in with cell memory; or (2) infused into an individual's mind. Thomas Edison, for instance, was continually being infused with ideas and plans that culminated in many innovations that helped the world. And although he was a great artisan and painter, Leonardo da Vinci was another who was infused with countless concepts, as is evident from his many drawings and blueprints of new inventions, several of which came to fruition.

In lots of cases, great artisans, inventors, musicians, and the like found or came up with something on the Other Side and then brought that knowledge down here with them. So some scientists with past knowledge in their cell memory and subconsciousness reincarnated into a scenario where they could use their talents again. Others made up their charts so that at a certain time or place they'd become infused with the necessary knowledge or idea and then used their talents to make it a reality on Earth. For example, Francine says that Marie Curie, who discovered radium, had been working on it at Home, and then she chose a life in which she'd be a scientist. She also asked that the rest of her project be infused in her before her death.

Many entities on the Other Side will go to the Hall of Research to learn or just observe the abundant wondrous projects going on that lead to discoveries, or what Francine calls "making better what has already been discovered." And on an individualistic basis, she says that these researchers try to get our guides to encourage us to have our hearts, lungs, and blood checked more often. Sadly, we don't listen most of the time. Yes, we're charted for certain things, but we don't have to take an early exit point unless we've just had enough. No matter what we contract in the way of illness or disease, if our will doesn't break, we can combat any- and everything.

What can seem confusing is that the Other Side is also researching so-called destructive things such as guns, explosives, and drugs. My guide explains that guns, for instance, weren't developed for war; rather, they were given to humans in the Middle Ages so they could hunt more extensively, thus providing more sustenance for their families. Gunpowder and other explosives were meant for pleasure (fireworks) and mining, while drugs were created for their curative properties. I've personally never been a fan of hunting for sport. I guess this makes me a bit of a hypocrite because I do eat fish, chicken, turkey, and beef; but I can't see where killing wild animals for trophies is beneficial. I also think that we have enough domesticated animals that we can use for food without having to kill them in the wild.

What our world does with the wonderful discoveries that come to us from beyond the veil can often be tragic. Take the atomic bomb, which was first researched to show the makeup of matter and whether or not it could be changed for the benefit of humankind. So what do we do? We put the elements together in a more combustible way to create something that has the capacity to destroy innumerable living things. In a small way, it's like taking a priceless Ming vase and hitting someone over the head with it—not only do you break something that's priceless, but you *take* a priceless life in the process.

Many of the scientists involved in the atomic-bomb project regretted it until the day they died, as I'm sure they didn't want it unleashed on the world in such a destructive manner. Proponents will always say that the bomb saved thousands of lives by bringing the war with the Japanese to a close, but did humankind actually learn anything in the process?

I wonder why the Americans didn't invite the Japanese, who probably already knew about the bomb anyway, to view its destructive power and negotiate peace with only the *threat* of destruction. I mean, we know that such a threat can be a deterrent, as nuclear powers around the world have refrained from annihilating each other and the rest of us . . . at least so far. Maybe this couldn't have been done with the Japanese at the time, but it seems to me that it would have been a viable alternative to just killing and maiming thousands of innocent people in Hiroshima and Nagasaki.

Yes, these events are charted, but we also have to take into consideration that dark-souled entities can take beautiful and beneficial things and make them evil or destructive. After all, it seems that our planet runs on trial and error, with the emphasis on *error*.

I realize that sometimes we need poison to kill poison—think of a deadly snakebite, which needs the reptile's venom in the antidote to combat the ravages of the bite—but to use something good for the purpose of evil always has karmic repercussions. Karma is absolutely enacted in life, and if we watch closely, a wrong done by someone who hurts another with the firm intention of doing harm will cause something similar to happen to him or her in about five years or less. It's as if a veil descends on wrongdoers, and they receive as much as, or more than, they gave out.

I will never forget the story my grandmother told me concerning karma. It seems that her family had a neighbor who would go out and hunt raccoons, and he was especially fond of capturing the creatures and bringing them home to boil them alive. Several years later, my grandmother learned that the neighbor had been working in a factory with large vats of boiling oil, and he'd fallen in one of them. Karma strikes again! While it may not have happened in five years, Grandma Ada said, "Close enough!"

Francine says that not only can you come up with new ideas and concepts in the Hall of Research, but you can also find records dating as far back as the invention of the wheel, which can be very interesting from a historical standpoint. In addition, she reports that the building is divided into what we'd refer to as "branches" of research, such as medicine, physics, music, the arts, electronics, and on and on it goes. It's a very big temple, but again, the physics of the Other Side are hard for us to understand while we're in life. Much like the old statement of "fitting 100 angels on the head of a pin," there can be many people in a space beyond the veil without any sense of being crowded. I think it's because our bodies are still dense and solid over there, but they don't have the thickness that our earthly shells have. I don't mean that we're fat or heavy on Earth, but our Home doesn't have the same type of physics that this world has.

Along with our bodies, Francine says that the reality of the Other Side makes its whole environment more solid and real. This says a lot to me about the earthly plane being a place of illusion, or as Plato once argued, we are nothing more than the shadows on the wall of a cave.

When we worry about our planet being destroyed, we must remember that it's not our true habitat. Our Home basically has Earth's same topography, with meadows, oceans, deserts, mountains, forests, and wide expanses of land; but all the ugliness, such as strip malls and factories, has been taken out, and the two "lost" continents of Atlantis and Lemuria have been added back in. Yet somehow we all fit together better over there. Once again, it can be very difficult for us to comprehend all of this here.

Getting back to the Hall of Research, my guide notes that each department is abuzz with ideas, mathematical tables, and plans and drawings—from airplanes, bridges, and skyscrapers to the tiniest of electronic components. And experiments in laboratories are constantly taking place without the need for animals because cell replication is commonplace and can literally be thought into being.

In fact, we can think anything into being on the Other Side, whether it be a building or a tiny microscopic cell (although most entities only tend to think their homes into existence). Just as we can change our outward appearance into another countenance for purposes of recognition, our minds are so powerful over there that we can actually create matter in a very real form. Now do you know why I call all of us miniature Gods?

As Francine has always said, "If you ask the question, then the answer can be given, but no answer is forthcoming to a question not asked." The problem most times is to figure out what question to ask. So many times, even in my society's research trances, subjects have been explored, but not enough time was devoted to them or they weren't delved into enough. This isn't anyone's fault, since my time for trance is limited—and time can be a great enemy when you're trying to extract information from a potentially unlimited source. I can only say that I'll continue to try my best to get as much as possible to you, in order to help you with your spiritual development and knowledge . . . after all, that's why I chose this life.

As I keep learning more about these temples on the Other Side, I become even more amazed at all the aid our Creators have made available to the entities beyond the veil, as well as to those of us still in life. I feel blessed to be one of the messengers to give out information, not only about our Creators Themselves, but also about how They have made us a part of Their existence and how much They love and care for us.

I know that I haven't spent much time on God the Father yet (but I will in a later chapter). Please be aware, however, that while the Mother God is very active and prominent and interacts constantly among us, Father God's actions, grace, love, and constant presence make everything as it is. Our all-perfect, all-loving, all-forgiving, and all-knowing Father is the Source from which all knowledge flows. We exist because of Him, our beloved Father and Co-Creator. He is never changing and always there for all of us, just as our blessed Mother is. They are the mortar that holds us firmly together, forever and always.

Francine once told me something that I find very fascinating, which is that while Jesus visits all the temples and is always on call, he does love to spend time in the Hall of Research. This surprised me at first, and then I began to think about his travels to India, Turkey, and France; and I came to realize that he was always interested in religion and theology. Being a special messenger for our Creators doesn't limit his knowledge of almost everything, but Francine says he loves to see how people are dealing with their beliefs and spirituality, along with their theology studies.

As for us "mere mortals," the Hall of Research is a fascinating place to visit. Just like with the other sites mentioned in this book, we can get to it in dreams via the astral state, or through meditation. I've had clients come back from the hall and then invent something, while others have found themselves suddenly interested in archaeology or other sciences.

When I personally visited this temple for the first time, I wanted to know about the pyramids, so I contacted an archaeologist who told me that they were made by UFOs. I was just blown away, yet the more I researched them, the more I began to see that this was indeed the truth. Later when I was watching a TV program about the Peruvian structures, one of the archaeologists featured said that there was no one who could have done this except someone from outer space. I was blown away again.

I've also discovered things that didn't come to pass until years later. For example, I said more than 40 years ago that we were in a polar tilt. And then many replied, "She's a very nice person, but she's kind of crazy." Now we know that thanks to global warming, we are absolutely in a type of polar tilt.

While you're at this temple, you might want to make sure that the method of determining when there's a physical problem in your body is implanted in your mind, along with the solution. I had a client who did this, for instance, and she found out that her hypothalamus gland was off. None of the numerous doctors she'd previously consulted knew this—the answer was discovered when she was in the Hall of Research during a meditation. After her general practitioner confirmed the diagnosis, he asked her how she'd learned this, and she just said, "I happened to get it in thought." I guess she didn't want to tell him that she'd gone to the Other Side to discover the cause of her illness.

If a loved one has a disease for which there's no cure on Earth yet, visiting the Hall of Research can help as well. If you're given information about treatments that aren't being used on this planet, make sure you consult with a physician about them. Also, you inventors or scientists out there might be surprised to know what you can access by visiting this temple. Who knows—maybe you were meant to read this book and visit this site to get some infusion for a new project or something else you've been working on.

I believe you should go to this temple many times because you can never learn too much. Even though some of the things you bring back may seem fantastic, be sure to write them down in a journal. You might be surprised that what you discovered comes to pass in five or ten years. (To reach this hall through meditation, please turn to page 215 after reading the instructions on pages 181–184.)

❀ ❀ ❀

Chapter 13

THE HALL
OF NATURE

Because the temples on the Other Side are not autonomous unto themselves, we can learn something from each and every one of them. All knowledge is shared, and no one has to worry about patents or plagiarism . . . it's truly "all for one, and one for all." However, some of the halls are more useful for research, and much like the temple from the last chapter, the Hall of Nature is one of them. Medical researchers have been known to work with this temple more than others for cures; and it also assists scientists working in the areas of biology, the environment, food supply, nutrition, agriculture, and so on.

Of course, given my love of animals, this is one of my favorite sites to tell you about. The Hall of Nature is devoted to the studies of animal husbandry, horticulture, marine life, and the environment. In comparison to the other temples, it's not that big, but it can easily accommodate the studies conducted inside. What's unique here is not the building itself, but rather what lies behind it.

You see, in back of the Hall of Nature are huge compounds that contain virtually every natural habitat for both plants and animals. There are various types of wooded areas—from sweltering rain forests to large stands of evergreens and all those that fall in between, such as mangrove swamps with towering hardwood trees that rival the Everglades. There's also every kind of topography you can think of, including mountains, deserts, plains, lakes, and oceans; and all the vegetation that has ever existed thrives here.

Among these compounds one can spot any species of animal, bird, reptile, and fish that has ever been, including the dodo and all types of dinosaurs. There are certainly numerous areas on the Other Side that are home to all the creatures, but this is almost like a living museum that's concentrated on the diverse collection of habitats, thus giving researchers the opportunity to study all the wonderful flora and fauna in their natural state.

The entities on the Other Side who work with animals use the Hall of Nature to find fresh ways to assist them, as well as to discover new medicines and treatments to help all the creatures on Earth. I must interject here to tell you that when we're Home, our communication with animals is much better than it is down here—we can actually link with them telepathically and understand their behavior; and they understand us, too. Now I'm not saying that they talk like in *The Chronicles of Narnia* because most of their thoughts are instinctual in nature, with an outpouring of love; however, if we project that we'd like them to lie down and be quiet, for instance, they'll do just that.

Because there's no need for sleep, food, or reproduction on the Other Side, animals don't have the need to protect their territory or fight for provisions. They all cohabit in perfect harmony without combating or eating each other, so we can witness lions and other predators playing with what would be their prey on Earth. Some of the most magnificent sights we can see on the Other Side are huge herds of wild game frolicking freely. And we can walk among them without fear and even pet them if we like.

Residents enjoy visiting the many jungles and plains where all these animals live and roam, and where they can be viewed playing in their natural habitats. These souls also love to watch the various types of dinosaurs, and most are still fascinated by how big they are.

Now so many people over the years have asked me if their pets were at Home, and of course the answer is yes. Let's be logical here—everything God makes is over there, including all the pets that we've ever loved, and they come to meet us when we cross over. In fact, Francine once told me that the people who love me on the Other Side can hardly get to me when I come back from a life because of all the animals who are there to greet me. It's like when you return from a trip and your furry friends practically knock you down and lick you to death because they're so happy that you're home.

The animals we've lost to death can also come back to visit us on this plane. One of my ministers who lost her cat, for instance, still feels him jump on her bed. To lose a pet is a heart-wrenching experience, and I've gone through it just like many of you have. I was so glad when Francine told me that domesticated animals are cared for in what we might call "homey" environments on the Other Side, since I feel that they are God's purest creations. I have five dogs, and whenever I don't feel well, they lie near me very quietly, as if they know what I'm going through and only want to give me their warm, positive energy. They are my angels right here on Earth.

Our precious pets want nothing from us except love, and that's just what they give back to us, unconditionally. We can be sick, worried, or cranky, yet they still adore us with unfailing loyalty. I believe that animals only become vicious if they're mistreated or if someone encroaches on their territory. I've always felt that mean dogs have been bred and trained by humans to be cruel and vicious, so you really can't blame them.

Francine says that the attack on magician Roy Horn (of Siegfried and Roy) by his white tiger Montecore was not as it seemed— the tiger was actually trying to save Roy, as it thought the magician was in danger and tried to carry him to safety. The reason I've inserted this here is because I've heard a few people speculate that Montecore was Roy's mother in a past life. That's just not true, for we don't incarnate into animals. The tiger was simply trying to protect Roy, who also felt this was the case and never had Montecore destroyed.

My beloved psychic grandmother said that animals see spirits that humans can't. I find it fascinating that my dogs will suddenly stare at the ceiling or over in the corner—and I'm wary of people whom they shun because I trust that they're picking up on some negative energy. I've known for a long time that animals can detect illness, even cancer, and science is now finding that out. I'm reminded of a friend of mine's dog, who would put his nose right up to her left eye and lick it whenever he came near. At first she thought it was funny . . . until she checked it out with her doctor, who found a small tumor behind her eye. She was lucky in that it wasn't cancerous, for if she'd waited much longer, it could have been.

Now while animals do have souls and are pure in nature, they are different creations and therefore don't have the same *type* of souls that we do. So we don't incarnate as animals or any other living thing; that is, there is absolutely no transmigration of the soul. We are who we are, and while we may live many lives, we're always human beings. Animals, however, only have one life, and their purpose has always been to aid humankind, whether as beloved pets, as aids in work or hunting, or as food. Having said that, I don't believe in using animals for experimentation.

Then there are our totem animals, who protect us when we incarnate and are right there to greet us when we first come Home. I currently have an elephant protecting me in this life, and a friend of mine has a cobra watching out for her. Once when she was walking to her car in a dark parking lot, a man jumped out at her, and she called on her totem. She swears that she instantly saw this gigantic snake rise in front of her, facing the man with its hood spread and hissing. She says the man's eyes got as big as silver dollars, and he ran away—no one will ever convince her that he didn't see her totem just as she did.

So in addition to your angels, guide, loved ones who have passed over, Jesus Christ, and Mother and Father God, you also have your totem looking out for you . . . once again, you can see that you're never alone. Just call on your totem when you feel afraid, and it will protect you.

And if you're wondering how to find out what your totem animal is, one of the best ways to do so is to ask your spirit guide during meditation. Also, most people who have an affinity for a certain animal will find that it is usually their totem.

Not only are there biologists studying animals at the Hall of Nature, but botanists, experts in horticulture, and ecologists also work with every kind of plant or tree imaginable there. Horticulturists plant flowers and interbreed different species to create new hybrids that are so gorgeous that they can never be described in earthly terms. The people who are working or researching in other temples often come here because of the incredible foliage and flowers . . . not to mention the aviaries, fisheries, and other animal habitats.

Botanists also investigate the properties of different plants, using advanced techniques in grafting, hydroponics, and experimental genetic manipulation to make new varieties and species of vegetation to maximize their potential—and to discover curative treatments that can help us on Earth. Francine says that everything these scientists work on creates new medicine; in fact, she has always contended that within plant life found in the Amazon, Peru, and certain islands lies the remedy for every malady or illness known to human or animal.

Think about how common mold led to the discovery of penicillin or how saw palmetto helps in the treatment of prostate problems. Then there's Librium, which has been used in a natural liquid form for years by Edgar Cayce's Association for Research and Enlightenment (ARE) to relieve stress. Compounds using the plant feverfew are found in some headache medications, aspirin comes from willow bark, and valerian root relaxes us.

If we know all this, why aren't we open to natural medicine? Don't get me wrong—I do get physicals, and God did make doctors—but we've become too dependent on pills and fast fixes in this society. It's just common sense to steer clear of sugar and too many carbohydrates if we're prone to diabetes, for instance, or to refrain from poisoning our livers and kidneys with too much alcohol. Sadly, we've become so overwhelmed and starved for spirituality that we try to fill our loneliness with food and booze. The longing we have for God and the Other Side can't be appeased like this, so we must try to eat healthfully and drink in moderation.

I know I push protein a lot, but Francine keeps saying that human beings are protein entities who have canine teeth, not flat ones. I don't believe that we should only eat big fat portions of red meat three times a day, but there is fish, turkey, chicken, or tofu—whatever keeps our diets higher in protein than carbohydrates, which are then converted into sugar. This doesn't mean that fruits and vegetables can't be part of our diets, but we must make them total less than our protein because we can't build bodies without bricks and mortar, so to speak.

Many of those with immune-deficiency illnesses such as AIDS are actually helped by all-protein diets for a few months, then gradually adding in only green veggies and a supplement containing all the necessary vitamins and minerals, especially the antioxidants. I've always used Centrum because it has everything I need, and I don't have to take individual and expensive pills. I'm not a brand-name or commercial person, but it's just ridiculous to take handfuls of vitamins or minerals unless you're treating some ailment that requires large doses.

One woman I talked to recently was taking 40 supplements *a day*. Well, sometimes you can do more harm than good to yourself, as some vitamins negate others, and your body will just flush them out. In addition, excessive amounts of vitamins A and D can stand in your liver and become toxic, and too much vitamin E makes your blood thin. So always ask your doctor or health-care provider about dosages, but use your common sense as well. Yes, lecithin is great for back problems and vitamin C helps colds, but some people just go crazy with every supplement they hear about. For example, keep in mind that there isn't a safe diet pill yet (although there will be in the next year or so—it will be a natural one that will affect the hypothalamus gland). Nothing beats eating right and watching your calories, so stop taking in all those sugars and quit gorging yourself. You don't need that much food to exist with health and vitality.

It's interesting that animals don't get fat when left to their own devices. However, when we feed them many times a day or give them what *we* eat, they gain weight and start suffering from our same illnesses, such as cancer, diabetes, and heart problems . . .

shouldn't that tell us something? When I've gone to Kenya, I've never seen an overweight native or a fat wild animal, except for maybe hippos. Of course, they walk, move, run, and dance all the time, while we in the "civilized world" sit and eat and drink ourselves right into obesity and death. Luckily, those entities working at the Hall of Nature are trying to wake us up to all of this.

(If you'd like to reach this temple through meditation, please turn to page 219 after reading the instructions on pages 181–184.)

❀ ❀ ❀

Chapter 14

THE TEMPLE OF
ARTISTIC ENDEAVOR

The Temple of Artistic Endeavor is probably one of the most beautiful halls visually, as it exudes so many colors—green, purple, pink, blue, and gold. It's Romanesque in design but only has two gigantic columns framing the front entrance, and it's octagon shaped with different wings coming out of the sides.

This building contains scale models of villages or types of architecture that have long been lost to us in the modern world, along with cave drawings, creations from ancient Egypt, and artifacts we haven't even heard of that go back to humankind's very beginning. But what's most exciting is that this hall houses the originals of all of Earth's famous paintings and works of art, such as Michelangelo's *David* and many statues of the ancient gods and goddesses. Now you may ask how these originals could be on the Other Side as well as down here. Well, all of the renowned artists either came up with these creations before or after they incarnated; therefore, what's stored in the Temple of Artistic Endeavor *are* originals and may deviate slightly from what we see on Earth (for example, the Venus de Milo has her arms intact).

Yet this hall isn't just an art museum or warehouse, since various artisans create at different "stations" throughout the building. Some are drafting large architectural projects; others are making gorgeous jewelry with every kind of gem you could name, as well as some that have yet to be discovered; and still others are painting, sculpting, writing, making pottery, illustrating, and even designing clothes.

Among those working in this hall are cabinetmakers, woodworkers, and craftspeople who employ all varieties of marble and stone. All of the elements are used to make beautiful art, much of which is ensconced in the buildings and private homes on the Other Side. Every type of craft and artistic work that you could ever conceive of is also in the Temple of Artistic Endeavor, and much of it hasn't even been infused to our planet yet. Some of the greatest painters, such as Raphael, Michelangelo, Vermeer, Leonardo da Vinci, Pablo Picasso, Claude Monet, Vincent van Gogh, Rembrandt van Rijn, Anthony Van Dyck, and Auguste Renoir do their work there; but there are also many talented individuals whom we on Earth have never heard of who nevertheless put out wonderful work. There are countless artists who were never recorded by our planet's history, yet they're quite renowned on the Other Side.

Another wing of the hall features music being composed by classical masters such as Franz Liszt, Claude Debussy, Johann Sebastian Bach, Ludwig van Beethoven, and Wolfgang Amadeus Mozart; as well as more modern figures like Nat King Cole, John Lennon, Cole Porter, Irving Berlin, Oscar Hammerstein, Jimi Hendrix, and countless others. There are drummers, guitar players, piano virtuosos, and so many thousands you haven't heard of who go back to their work when their earthly lives are over. There are also arrangers, producers, lyricists, actors, and directors still practicing their art. John Ford and John Wayne, for instance, are still great pals on the Other Side. The Gershwin brothers, Glenn Miller, Buddy Holly, and Bobby Darin are still doing what they love to do. Elvis Presley was a fixture at this temple until he wanted to come back to Earth and go into gospel music primarily, so he incarnated again around 2002.

Groups get together and perform all the time beyond the veil. Musicians have jam sessions or just practice with one another, from the great orchestras to the smaller jazz ensembles. The symphonies are spectacular, for not only is the music very celestial, but new compositions are played frequently and mixed in with the classic pieces that we know of on the Earth plane. Beloved standards from Broadway shows are also played often, as are new works from talented composers. Francine has told me that Richard Rodgers works with both Oscar Hammerstein and Lorenz Hart, and they've all come up with some wonderful musicals. In addition, the famous team of Lerner and Loewe is working together again and putting out beautiful work as well.

Musicians on the Other Side play every conceivable type of instrument, from old "celestas" to zithers, oboes, pianos, violins, tubas, drums, guitars, and horns of every kind—and if you can think of an instrument, there's someone who excels at it. Everyone plays all types of music, from flamenco to classical, but strangely enough there's no call for rap or hip-hop. My guide says that's because such genres are indigenous to Earth and were born out of its negativity. In the perfect environment of our Home, the use of swear words is unnecessary, and lyrics about violence and misogyny aren't relatable. Hard rock and heavy metal are also associated with our planet's problems and not played over there, but good old rock 'n' roll is enjoyed by many, as is pop and easy listening.

Now for those of you who like rap and heavy metal, understand that when your mind opens up to full capacity in a perfect environment with no negativity, you'll find that there's no need for music or art to reflect that negativity. You may think the Other Side is all about "elevator music," but let me assure you that it isn't—there are many lively compositions that many enjoy. The pieces are very diverse and reflect all cultures, from the Indian raga to the Irish jig.

In fact, the performing arts are well represented over there; and plays, concerts, musicals, and movies are constant sources of entertainment. There are also acrobats, jugglers, magic performers, dancers, and people in all forms of entertainment working, practicing, and studying in the Temple of Artistic Endeavor. There's a section for set designers, lighting experts, screenwriters, and animators . . . not to mention an entire area for makeup and costume design. (People often don't realize that the art of makeup goes back to ancient Egypt and Greece.) Edith Head, who used to be one of the greatest costume designers for movies, is often seen in this temple.

So many famous writers and poets, such as Plato, William Shakespeare, Herman Melville, Dorothy Parker, Percy Bysshe Shelley, John Keats, Elizabeth Barrett Browning, Henry Wadsworth Longfellow, Edgar Rice Burroughs, Robert Louis Stevenson, Jack Kerouac, Pearl Buck, Ernest Hemingway, John Steinbeck, and endless others still create in this temple.

In addition, all the writers, composers, and painters freely help out their fellow artists, or provide information and training to anyone who wants it. So people who work in the Hall of Research, let's say, go to the Temple of Artistic Endeavor to see what they'd like to get involved in. Consequently, it wouldn't be unusual to find a microbiologist discovering a talent for the French horn.

Most of what we do on the Other Side is related directly to our themes, which we utilize to perfect our soul for greater spirituality, but that doesn't necessarily mean that all the lives we lead on Earth follow our main themes. For example, we may have an artistic theme and work in the Temple of Artistic Endeavor as a painter, but we choose to incarnate as an investment banker to perfect certain attributes and only paint as a hobby . . . or not have anything to do with it at all. (For more on our themes, please see my book *Spiritual Connections.*)

I think this may explain why so many of us are unhappy with our jobs; unfortunately, it often can't be helped because we need to put food on the table and a roof over our heads. But for those of us who have a strong yearning to do something that our current careers aren't satisfying, it might help to know that the urge could very well come from what we enjoy when we're Home.

Shortly after the salon in which Francine presented information about this hall, a woman who had been in attendance came to one of my book signings. She told me that she'd meditated and had found herself in the exquisite Temple of Artistic Endeavor and discovered that she'd always wanted to paint. Then she presented me with a watercolor of Azna, our Mother God. Now I have to tell you that I've received some very strange pictures over the years, but this one was truly lovely, with beautiful and almost unearthly colors that had a dreamlike quality to them. I thanked her, and she then related that she'd shown similar works to a representative from an art gallery, who was really interested. This woman was able to bring the ability to paint back with her, simply by tapping into her talent on the Other Side.

The Temple of Artistic Endeavor can help you find the inspiration to paint, write, play music, and on and on. You might think that your ideas come from dreams or a particular person or situation you've encountered—while this may be true in many instances, your creativity can also be sparked by visiting this hall. Maybe your passion is design, for instance, but your inspiration has been lagging. Well, if you can get to the Temple of Artistic Endeavor, you might be surprised by what you come back with, or what the experience will do for your own inspiration. Even if you just dabble in a hobby, a visit there could bring your abilities to new heights.

It's never too late; after all, think of Grandma Moses, who picked up a brush at 76 years of age and became a famous artist. Let's face it—doing things keeps us young. If we stop learning and moving, our brains will atrophy and our bodies will follow suit because they believe that we're already dead, so everything begins to shut down. Even if it's just baking, getting interested in crafts or gardening, or building things with our hands, this type of activity sets up a synaptic connection to remind our brains that we're alive and well. It doesn't really matter if what we've created is good or not, as the important thing is the act of creation itself.

Personally, I love crafts and do whatever I can in this area, since they keep my mind quiet yet active. Sometimes taking up a new hobby gives me a renewed vitality and interest in life. For example, I'll write like crazy, then stop and needlepoint or paint. Most people don't even realize that I can paint, but I actually began to do so after a visit to the Temple of Artistic Endeavor. It's very strange that I tend to paint in a Japanese-looking style.

I've even taught my granddaughter, Angelia, how to knit and needlepoint, and she has enjoyed doing both since she was five. Now a teenager, she's also a great writer who's been in charge of her school paper. You can say that all this comes from genetics, but my other grandchildren haven't taken on these pursuits the way she has. Of course her dad, my son Christopher, found that he has a talent for writing, too, and his two books (especially his latest, *My Psychic Journey*) have both done so well. Yet much of this depends on the individual. For example, I love crafts as much as my own grandmother did, but my sister, Sharon, never has. I'm not being critical here—it's just that my mother, who did nothing with her life, took over Sharon's as well.

This may cause you to ask, "But what about my chart?" Naturally you have your specific chart, but you can make it as positive or as much fun as you choose while still learning what you came here for. Your disposition plays a part here, as does your personality and soul's essence. So if you come into a beautiful artistic life that you picked but you just live it halfheartedly, you haven't taken full advantage of your chart. It's like getting a present and not opening it: You have it and might even know what it is, but you haven't taken it out and really enjoyed it.

Always remember that the important thing about life is not necessarily its direction, but how it is lived. Anyone can be a couch potato, but it takes courage to face life head-on and give it the energy, passion, and attention it deserves. That's why I recommend that you visit the Temple of Artistic Endeavor during a time when you feel depressed or down—it will do you a world of good. (If you'd like to do so through meditation, please turn to page 223 after reading the instructions on pages 181–184.)

♘ ♘ ♘

Chapter 15

THE TEMPLE
OF VOICES

The Temple of Voices is smaller than the other halls on the Other Side, yet it probably has the greatest acoustics of them all. The building is perfectly round, Romanesque in design, and all gold: The columns are gold, the steps are gold, the doors are gold, and the dome is gold. In fact, no other temple over there is totally gold like this one—yet it seems to be glowing with a tremendous iridescent, almost fuchsia-colored, light.

I think that this hall's round dimensions are what make the acoustics so perfect. When you enter, you immediately hear a montage of the most beautiful sounds because there's a small auditorium in the middle of the temple, surrounded by rooms for souls who are perfecting their voices, pitch, or arrangements. Here's where you'll find the great masters of all types of music; and they're only too happy to help you sing, play, or learn. They offer more intense training than what you'd get at the Temple of Artistic Endeavor, as this place is more for those who want to be masters themselves.

I know that it can seem as if these temples overlap, but there *are* differences between them. Not only is the Temple of Voices devoted exclusively to music in all its facets, but it's also where staged performances take place. It's true that all singers and musicians work in the Temple of Artistic Endeavor, but in this hall they're able to perform *and* get more instruction from masters.

Visiting the Temple of Voices is a very uplifting experience; in fact, Francine says that it attracts souls like a magnet because many who come in almost go into a state of rapture thanks to the tones and quality of the melodies. The hall is utilized by musicians of every type, from those who play older instruments such as the harpsichord to electric-guitar wizards. You'll also find the greatest singers practicing their art here, such as Enrico Caruso, Frank Sinatra, and Elvis Presley, who was a frequent visitor before he reincarnated.

The primary voices, however, are those of angels, whose purpose is to give praise to God and creation with their exquisite singing. In other words, the most important aspect of the Temple of Voices is that it's almost like the home base of the phyla of angels known as the "Cherubim" and "Seraphim," who are truly God's heavenly choir. As they're always singing there, their lovely voices continually permeate the entirety of the Other Side. They do have special new songs for high holy days, but all the songs are heard everywhere over there, and in many languages. You might think that would be aggravating, but you can tune it in or out.

"The angels' voices," Francine says, "sound as clear as bells, and they resonate." She explains that although you can listen to these beautiful Cherubim and Seraphim singing anywhere you go, it isn't loud. It's always a soothing background sound, unless you go into the Temple of Voices itself.

Another interesting aspect of this hall is the presence of a huge golden organ—which goes from ceiling to floor with giant pipes and four keypads—that emits a heavenly sound when played. It often accompanies the angels when they sing, and can be heard all over the Other Side, just like their voices.

The Cherubim and Seraphim also give what we might call concerts in this "Carnegie Hall" of the Other Side. While this site is certainly not the only place for performances, it *is* considered the best, so not only do the angels perform regularly there, but so do all of our Home's musicians and singers.

The performances at the Temple of Voices include all the operas, compositions, and songs that you can think of, as well as those you've never heard on Earth. Countless individuals come in with requests for particular pieces—and you may be wondering how it can be that if there are so many people in the temple, one person could hear only what he or she wants to. Well, that's another puzzle piece of the Other Side, which our earthly minds can't comprehend. Just know that God made this temple so that everyone can have his or her own private concert.

It brought tears to my eyes when Francine told me that my dad goes in there to ask for "Somewhere Over the Rainbow." You see, that was our song, and before he died, he told me that whenever I'd hear it down here, he'd be with me. Nevertheless, if I hear it right after I've been thinking about him, it gives me chills. Recently, for example, my son and I were on a Hay House cruise to Mexico when that song came on. It seemed like an odd time and place to be hearing it, and my son just looked at me and said, "Mom, Grandpa's here."

I also remember when I first came to California more than 45 years ago, and I was so homesick and in a miserable house *and* marriage. Then to top it off, my parents and sister came out from Kansas City and moved in with us, and I was the only one who had a job for nine months. I'd often have trouble sleeping at night, until I'd hear the most heavenly music that seemed to come from midair above me. And during a terrible time in her life, one of my ministers came home totally rejected . . . only to look up and see what looked like hundreds of angels with harps playing this absolutely Divine tune that lifted her spirits.

Francine tells me that these were soothing musical messages sent to us from the Other Side. My grandmother used to say that along with animals and children, music is one of God's gifts. She also said that if you find anyone who hates any of these things, be careful. I don't mean someone who just doesn't have a pet or a child, but actually *hates* them . . . those are dark entities. I think that whoever came up with the old adage "Music has charms to soothe the savage beast" was implying that the beasts were us humans here on Earth.

People, places, and events can so often be recalled by songs because music is like a color or even an emotion. Just take a second right now to remember what brings back your strongest romantic or sentimental memories. I, for one, can mark important times of my life by the music that was playing: Whenever I hear "Earth Angel," for example, I immediately think of being in love for the first time.

As I mentioned before, my father dedicated "Somewhere Over the Rainbow" to me, and every time I hear it, I vibrate with thoughts of him—along with the beauty of the song itself—from the roots of my hair clear down to my toes. This also happens when I hear "Clair de Lune," which was my grandmother's favorite—it brings back such memories and such a vibration in my soul that it's truly like being in an altered state. (I'm also convinced that along with music, smells or scents pull up the most intense recollections.)

Hopefully in meditation you'll get to visit the Temple of Voices, as so many have after Francine shared information about it in trance. Even if you haven't been musical in this life but always wanted to be—which, of course, could be coming from a past life or even a memory of Home—try going to this hall. When you eventually do pass over and would like to further explore your musical ability, you can do so at the place some on the Other Side call "the Temple of Tones." This is very interesting to me because over there we all have our own tone, our own aura, and of course, our own individuality.

People think that we change when we cross over, but we don't. For example, Francine says that my humor is the same and I still write and lecture. (Why is it that I felt at one point that I just wanted to go lie in a field for a while? I never could . . . that's not me.) We might be a better version of ourselves, but our base personality stays exactly the same. Thank God, otherwise we'd all be sickening robots.

(If you'd indeed like to reach this temple through meditation, please turn to page 227 after reading the instructions on pages 181–184.)

❧ ❧ ❧

Chapter 16

THE TEMPLE
OF LECTURES

The Temple of Lectures is a multileveled building surrounded by a golden gate and fence and topped by an orange dome. Even though it features columns and other Romanesque touches, it has a lot of Egyptian influences, including lotuslike designs at the tops of the pillars. There is also a large golden obelisk behind the hall, which represents the finger of God pointing upward and the channeling of lecture material from Him.

Much like the Temple of Artistic Endeavor instructs people in drama, this hall teaches individuals how to give a lecture, but it's also the home base for what we might refer to as the Other Side's "regular speakers." So the main portion of the hall has tiered, amphitheater-like seating for audiences and a section for teachers. Here, public-speaking experts help people with their delivery, for example, and give them instruction on topics such as how to hold an audience's attention and how to combine one's knowledge with humor.

Now there's another section of this temple where you'll find some of the greatest minds in science, math, medicine, inventions, politics, philosophy, music, and any other subject you can think of working and studying. Benjamin Franklin speaks here often, as do other eminent personages such as Jesus, Mohammed, Buddha, Aristotle, Socrates, Abraham Lincoln, Albert Einstein, Thomas Edison, Claude Monet, and Victor Hugo.

I think it's so wonderful that authors still write, actors still perform, and musicians still play on the Other Side. And what many study and then lecture about will be brought with them when they incarnate. In other words, nothing ends with the conclusion of earthly life; rather, we just continue where we left off at Home.

Upcoming concerts, lectures, or similar events that are held in the Temple of Lectures are posted in the Hall of Wisdom. Naturally, some speakers are more popular than others, but Francine says that she tries to attend most of the lectures given in this temple, spanning from Marie Curie to Elizabeth Barrett Browning. However, she loves to hear Benjamin Franklin speak because while he disseminates fascinating information and is politically and socially savvy, he's also quite funny. Mark Twain is another of her favorites because he's so witty and usually shares excerpts of whatever he's writing.

Francine also enjoys hearing from Georgia O'Keeffe, who was such a great artist and led a fascinating life, doing what she wanted in a time when women weren't supposed to be so free. My guide says that Mary Baker Eddy talks frequently; Dorothy Parker holds small and intimate intellectual salons with her friends; Mary Magdalene, who is a compelling orator, lectures quite often; and on and on it goes. This book couldn't possibly list all of the presenters over there, including those whom we on Earth have never heard of. Everyone has a story to tell, so many just get up and share their life stories and how they survived. Numerous great minds that history has neglected also share their experiences and culture.

Anyone is permitted to have a go at lecturing in this hall. Francine said that once *I* even gave a speech—on theology. I can't believe that I had the nerve to get up in front of all those souls, but you never know. Yes, I lecture on *this* side, but when you think of all the great minds I would have been speaking to over there, it's a little intimidating. Yet there's no such thing as stage fright on the Other Side, so people who have always wanted to share their ideas, poetry, plays, or what have you are only too happy to get up and address the masses without fear of being judged.

After each and every lecture, there's always time for questions and answers, and then the attendees often stand around and talk. It's much like what we on Earth do at art-gallery or museum galas. There's a lot to discuss, for as Francine has told me, most of what's presented in the Temple of Lectures is totally fresh, such as new ideas or musical compositions.

For example, in the course of a "day" (of course we know that there's no time beyond the veil), my guide says that she saw an original play by Shakespeare, heard a presentation from Socrates that blended philosophy and quantum physics, and went to a lecture on politics given by Thomas Jefferson. Then the various attendees all got together in groups to discuss what they'd seen and heard and do some brainstorming. I thought, *How glorious it must be to be in the presence of these great minds and totally absorb their concepts!*

Francine says that there are even new insights to be gained from old knowledge. For example, she recently heard a marvelous lecture given by Albert Einstein in which he offered a new explanation for the theory of relativity. She said that he confirmed what I've often said: *The only ones who understand quantum physics are the psychics or the prophets.* What Einstein was trying to convey is that time, space, and light converge into God's now and are all relative to each other, which is why he called it his "relativity theory." His theory has always sounded so convoluted and complex to me, but when he put it into these simplistic terms (which is the mark of a good teacher), it became very clear and easy to understand. Having my guide share this information was so enlightening for me.

Francine says that even if she doesn't necessarily care for what the lecturer is talking about, she's never heard a boring presentation. Everyone in the Temple of Lectures is dramatically knowledgeable, and coming here is an excellent way to learn about all subjects . . . even the ones Earth has yet to hear about. She insists that one day this new information will be infused into some capable recipients on our planet, and then it will come through to the entire world.

The Temple of Lectures is a beneficial place to visit if you struggle with public speaking or would just love to be in the audience when great minds are presenting. So before you go, ask that you get to see or hear Abraham Lincoln; Benjamin Franklin; Dr. Martin Luther King, Jr.; or anyone else who's of interest to you. And be sure to take along a notebook! (If you'd like to reach this temple through meditation, please turn to page 229 after reading the instructions on pages 181–184.)

※ ※ ※

Chapter 17

THE TEMPLE OF MYSTICAL TRAVELERS AND MISSION-LIFE ENTITIES

The Temple of Mystical Travelers and Mission-Life Entities is a fairly small building, and although it is Romanesque in design, it is fairly nondescript in comparison with some on the Other Side. In many ways it is a reflection of those it honors in the sense that a lot of mission-life entities and mystical travelers don't always get the recognition they deserve. However, this hall *is* very beautiful. The columns are silvery rather than gold, as is the temple's door and interior—the walls even seem to give off a silvery light. And, as its name implies, the purpose of this site is to help those who wish to become mystical travelers and mission-life entities.

What's the Difference Between the Two Groups?

— Becoming a **mission-life entity** is a very important decision and should not be taken lightly. Like the choice of being either a white or dark entity, this is done at the time of creation—it's an option that certain souls select to take on extra hardships or duties in life in order to advance more quickly. If a charted life for most people is challenging, it will be even more difficult for these individuals, but they know this from the beginning. No one is looked down on if they choose not to be a mission-life entity; after all, many white entities don't take on this role because so much is asked of them in their charts. It's like I recently told a client in a reading: "If you meet someone you love and admire, it doesn't matter whether they have their GED or a Ph.D." Sometimes the more simplistic we are, the happier we are.

When mission-life entities go back to the Other Side, they sort of float between all the levels. Of course everyone can do so over there, but these souls just continually research and reach all the levels, since I guess they want to experience everything more than anyone else does. And when these entities incarnate, it's so they can take on special assignments. They seem to come in with a purpose to make this a better world, whether it's through medicine, science, religion, politics, or the like.

While Mother Teresa; Abraham Lincoln; Billy Graham; and Dr. Martin Luther King, Jr., are examples of mission-life entities who have received acclaim for their work, such souls don't have to be popular or have their names in lights. Many have been heroes in war who go unnamed but nevertheless try to save our planet from some form of atrocity. The world may not know them, but God does.

As I tell my ministers, "Do all things without any hope of praise. Yes, it's nice to be recognized, but if you're searching for popularity, you're in for a fall. Let the skepticism of others rain down like arrows without any points. Those who know you will see your heart and soul because people are savvy and know if you truly love them." I had to learn this for myself early on. Yet no matter how tired I get sometimes, I love humanity and it is what keeps me going, just as it did with Thomas Edison, Jonas Salk, and so many others.

Mission-life entities are also open channels for infusion from the Other Side, thus bringing about betterment for God and humankind, yet they can be found everywhere and in every lifetime. They can even be in the entertainment field if they have strong morals or principles that they fiercely live by. In other words, they don't just profess to love Jesus or make movies with high morals but then live their lives contrary to these spouted beliefs; rather, they say what they mean and mean what they say.

Someone who shows one face to the public and then privately steals, cheats, take drugs, and so on is not a mission-life entity, but rather a wannabe who's just after fame and glory.

— The **mystical traveler** is similar to the mission-life entity, but in other ways is quite different. Mystical travelers have a more complex and demanding role than mission-life entities do, for it's the highest of spiritual callings and possibly the most difficult. Those who decide to become mystical travelers accept the numerous challenges that they will face upon incarnation, and they must take an oath to totally give up their will to God. As soon as they make this pledge, the mantle will fall upon their shoulders—and once it does, it can never be removed. Thus, it requires much thought, sincere dedication, and a willing loss of ego to take on this role.

Each individual is given the opportunity in his or her last life to take on the mantle of being a mystical traveler, which can be accepted or rejected without any shame or scorn. Speaking of last lives, they're more common now than ever before. This could mean that we're getting close to the end of "the reincarnation schematic," or the chance to incarnate, on this planet. In fact, I'm certain that we're coming to the end of times in about 95 years—the world will survive, but it won't be able to sustain life as we know it. However, we will have perfected our souls by that time and will no longer have a need for reincarnation, so maybe we'll go to other planets or just stay on the Other Side and keep on learning.

Now people who spend all their time in prayer may be mission-life entities, but they're not necessarily mystical travelers. You see, mystical travelers are always out in the thick of humanity and tend to be found teaching, leading, or are otherwise visible to the world. And not only do they perform great humanitarian acts, but they do so tirelessly and usually with no thought for themselves.

The charts of these very advanced souls are harder to read because unlike other entities, they can take extra unwritten measures in order to do more or go "beyond the call of duty." It isn't enough for them to just live a good life; they make tremendous sacrifices in order to help others. That's why I'm sure the Catholic Church made the category of *saint* for some of these people, as they didn't know what else to call them. I'm convinced that everyone on the Other Side is a mission-life entity or a saint anyway. There isn't just a Saint Francis or a Saint Christopher—it seems to me that *everyone* who makes it over there is a blessed and sacred soul.

Mystical travelers don't only come from theology- or faith-based backgrounds (although more do originate in this area than other occupations), but can be great scientists, doctors, lawyers, and teachers as well. Yet they do tend to be controversial; and their messages often fly in the face of our world's religions, politics, and laws. It's true that most, if not all, of the planets in the cosmos are not anywhere near as difficult or as hellish as is Earth—which is why so many mystical travelers have come here and are still coming. Strangely, as nightmarish as this world is, this is the only place where you can become a mystical traveler; in fact, Francine says that other planetary entities come here specifically to take on this role. I guess because Earth is such a horrendous place, it's a type of badge of honor to come here.

Then again, we regularly return the favor: My guide says that when our own mystical travelers finish their earthly lives, they're usually called to go to other galaxies or planets. They're truly the troubleshooters of creation, so they're required to go anywhere in the universe that needs help. Mystical travelers take up the causes of truth and healing and are committed to making things better, but they don't often have much of a life as we'd normally know it. Yes, they can be married and have children, but their main purpose is to try to handle everything they're asked to and to create harmony while multitasking.

It seems that these souls' paths are strewn with skepticism and cruelty and possibly even exile or death. (For example, Jesus was at the highest level of mystical traveler, as were many other messengers who have made their mark on the world. However, Francine says that Christ hasn't gone to other planets as far as anyone knows or has related to her, but she feels that he certainly could have.) These souls are often not appreciated in life as they should be—perhaps because they step away from the masses and see truths that others have yet to come upon. Many parts of their lives are in upheaval, but they persevere despite the rejection and loneliness.

Again, anyone can become a mystical traveler, but much thought and even prayer should be put into it because once the mantle drops, it cannot be removed by the individual. It's a solemn and unbreakable pact between a man or woman and the Mother God, which is written in gold in the Hall of Records. There has only been one person throughout time who had the mantle removed because he defected. I won't name him, but it was very pitiful to see, and the dramatic aftermath was even more karmic.

In fact, the pitfalls for mystical travelers are plentiful because it becomes easy for those in human form to get caught up in fame and power. Unlike mission-life entities, who usually have a singular purpose or life theme, mystical travelers can take on lives that are measured in different degrees from one to six, with six being the highest (and which includes the level of messiahs). These levels don't really matter, though—what does matter is that they've given up their will to God, so their paths are very, very difficult and quite pronounced in their spirituality.

So as I've said, if you don't think you can perform this role, don't even try. It would be much better for you to live your life and love God, do good, and go Home. You will still progress and be loved just as much.

Now please don't ever believe, even for one moment, that mystical travelers or mission-life entities are better or more advanced than anyone else in our Creators' eyes, for They truly love all of Their creations equally. Yes, it's important to stretch one's soul, but a person who takes care of animals or plants is just as important to, and cherished by, our Parents as anybody else. Here again, we human beings tend to indulge in anthropocentrism—that is, giving our human traits to Mother and Father God. So we believe that if *we* are capable of anger, jealousy, and favoritism, then They must be as well . . . which just isn't true. We've adopted a false concept of our Creators possessing moods or emotions, rather than understanding that both Mother and Father God's makeup is simply love. They love us unconditionally, which means that They are constantly forgiving and merciful, no matter what we do or how many mistakes we make.

Our earthly emotions are certainly reflected by our beliefs— look at how many diverse religions there are, for instance, and how each one in some way is in opposition to all the others. A judgment such as "My God is the true God and better than your God" is always tainted because it's based on our human values. Consequently, our perceived concepts of God are constantly at odds . . . and ultimately wrong.

Look at history, for example: Kings and queens and emperors, who were at the highest level of our social structure, were many times considered to be gods. Even today we deify certain individuals—we tend to idolize the world's most rich, famous, powerful, beautiful, talented, and charismatic men and women. We all have our heroes, and those who don't feel the same as we do become enemies of a sort because they may not like Tiger Woods and instead adore Jack Nicklaus, for instance.

If you can't resist judging those who have fame, education, beauty, talent, or wealth, your own spiritual growth will be threatened. I have met uneducated shamans in Africa who possess more wisdom in their little fingers than some Ph.D.'s. I know housekeepers who are more kind, loving, and giving than most movie stars I've encountered. In other words, don't judge a book by its cover. To be truly spiritual and at one with God, you must accept life as it is and work within it to make it better. There are always going to be rich people and poor people. There are always going to be wars, just as there will be times of peace. There are always going to be different cultures, races, moralities, laws, and traditions. You're not necessarily going to be able to change things to the way you think they should be, but you *can* change them for the better in some small way.

Start thinking about what's best for everyone instead of what's best for yourself. Keep an open mind and listen to others, for certain individuals may be able to help you learn and gain wisdom.

And most important, try to treat all those you meet with love and kindness even though you might not agree with them—we have enough discord and negativity on this planet already, and we don't need to make more. It's okay to agree to disagree. Don't judge the souls of others, for you have no idea what roads they've traveled (but you can certainly avoid those whom you feel can contaminate your soul).

Finally, when it comes to the perceived "favoritism" of God that many religions put forth, I have a few points to make. While our Father and Mother don't have favorites and do love us all unconditionally and equally, that doesn't mean that They created everyone equally. If They did, we'd all be clones or robots, each acting the same as one another. Look at nature, in which all of the different species have strengths and weaknesses. One animal might have the gift of camouflage to protect it from its enemies, while another might possess great speed or an armored shell—but they're *not* all created the same, which contributes to their own uniqueness. It's the same with human beings.

Souls such as Jesus Christ, Buddha, Mohammed, and other very evolved beings had to be created to be leaders for the rest of us . . . and this was our Creators' doing, not theirs. Jesus certainly had no say in how he was created—Mother and Father God chose to make him the way They did for a particular purpose, just as Mary Smith in Anywhere, U.S.A., was made for a purpose. This doesn't necessarily make Jesus more or less endearing to God than Mary Smith, but *somebody* had to be Jesus Christ, just as somebody had to be Mary Smith.

Again, we human beings tend to judge a person's worth by his or her stature, but our Creators do not. That's why we'd be mistaken to think that a mystical traveler or mission-life entity is more loved by Them than we are. Yes, there are entities who are more evolved than others, just as we have different traits and personalities that are different from others, but that doesn't mean that such individuals are the "chosen ones."

Here's an analogy you might relate to: Let's say you have two children, and after high school one goes to college and gets an engineering degree, while the other becomes a grocery clerk.

Would their level of education or type of job make any difference to you as far as how much you loved them? Of course not. Well, it's the same thing with our Creators. The one thing that They have given to all of Their created entities is *potential,* which means that all souls can go as far spiritually as they want to.

So if we learn and work hard enough, there's no reason why we couldn't reach or even surpass the progression of any other entity on the planet. While some individuals were given the innate wisdom and spirituality to be leaders, that knowledge and maturity can (and hopefully will) be attained by us all eventually. That's why we seek to perfect our souls. It's not for us; rather, we do it for our Creators and to be closer to Them. All of us have the potential to be highly evolved individuals, so our goal should be to help others attain their own chosen state of evolvement. Some of us might prefer to honor and love our Parents by giving to others, entering the priesthood, or helping the poor or needy—but we'll all become very advanced entities in our own time and place.

(If you'd like to reach the Temple of Mystical Travelers and Mission-Life Entities through meditation, please turn to page 233 after reading the instructions on pages 181–184.)

❧ ❧ ❧

Chapter 18

THE TEMPLE OF SPIRIT GUIDES

This temple is fairly plain compared to many of the others. While the building does have gold pillars and doors, the rest of it is made up of unadorned gray marble. Inside is just a huge hall with a large podium and rows of built-in chairs, much as you'd find in a movie theater. Lining the hall are what are called the "compatibility meeting rooms," in which people meet their spirit guides and decide if they're compatible with the individuals' missions or charts.

All spirit guides have to study for many years in our time to be able to know their charges' charts backward and forward, and they need to possess the abilities to help and keep up. If they don't understand or are puzzled by something, there are classes they can take or individual counselors or Council members to help them.

Psychic Ruth Montgomery called them the "nudging companions along the way," which they are, but they're also so much more than that. Spirit guides are far better than any friends we could ever have—we can get mad at them, ignore them, or try to release them, but they remain steadfast in their duties. (The only beings who don't have guides are dark entities, but I'm sure that's because their whole mission is to seek and destroy and make everyone else's lives miserable.)

Usually Council members will meet you at the Temple of Spirit Guides to help you choose one. They advise you as to who would fit best with you, as far as protection and advice is concerned. A guide's personality and disposition are also important because having true compatibility is vital in helping you fulfill your chart.

After you choose your spirit guide, he or she studies your chart and then meets with you to meticulously go over it together. Your guide will also help you enter into your earthly life. This entity will be with you from birth until death, never wavering in watchfulness and caring, and always cognizant of what you need. Your guide will keep up with your chart constantly, and although he or she can't interfere with it, your guide can certainly help make it easier and bring you some comfort. Your guide will make appeals to the Council for you and even petition Mother God to intervene if necessary, and will convene with other guides to talk over problems and give each other advice, as well as calling upon angels for assistance or sending for more guardians in times when you need extra protection.

It's important to note here that angels have no duties, knowledge, or input in your life—they're only healers and protectors and just go where they're told to. Unlike angels, your spirit guide has gone through at least one earthly existence and is privy to information that they're not. Your guide is the real coordinator of your life, while angels have to be directed. Even if they come into physical form, it's because they've been pointed to a particular mission.

Francine has told me that I wasn't too thrilled to have her as my spirit guide. Apparently I thought she was too stiff, but the Council convinced me that I needed her. They said that while I was outgoing and very loving, I was too trusting, so I needed a more serious and scholastic guide for my mission in this life. So far it has worked out fine because she's been a loving and trusted friend (although I sometimes wish she had a better sense of humor). Francine has indeed been a great balance for my impulsiveness and temper and has always been there for me in times of trouble. Also, her name is really Iena, but she's never gotten mad at me for calling her Francine. I love her dearly.

One of the problems involved in communicating with guides on the Other Side is that they usually answer questions literally. Francine is getting much better at this, but I remember that when she first started coming into me in trance, she was literal to a fault. A question such as "Should we have a garage sale?" for instance, would elicit an answer like "Why would you want to sell your garage?" Or when she was asked if an individual had told others about a particular incident, she would say, "Yes, he was a bird on a chair." What she meant was that he was a stool pigeon. God love her—she didn't mean to be funny, but it took her a while to pick up on our idioms and slang.

She also had a tendency early on not to expand on her answers. So if you asked her, "Will I ever get married?" she'd simply reply, "Yes," with no further detail. I will say that she learned very quickly and is now quite polished in responding to questions, and she elaborates as needed. I really can't fault her for not volunteering more than she does, however, because she's not a mind reader. Also, with all the information she has at her disposal, where would she start? We've tried to stick to one or two subjects in our research trances, and she's been a wondrous source for us, but we always have to remember that she can't give answers to questions that haven't been asked.

As she told me years and years ago, "If you can ask the question, you can have the answer." The hell of that is we don't always know which question to ask. I'm sure that if someone hadn't inquired about the temples on the Other Side in that salon we had a few months ago, we might never have discovered what has resulted in the book you're holding in your hands. Francine has volunteered information over the years, but she says that she waits for human spirituality to grow and then gives me what we're ready to handle. It reminds me of how parents don't offer to tell children about "the birds and the bees" until they're old enough or mature enough to ask. It does make me wonder at times what I haven't asked my guide or what I *could* ask. I've finally given up and accepted that the answers will come when she feels the time is right.

Yes, I've gotten angry at Francine at times—I've argued with her, asked her where she was, and accused her of being on vacation. Of course all of this is silly because I'm the one who picked this sometimes hellish chart, not her. Through all of our years together, I've also learned what a faithful and loyal friend she's been, as well as the myriad things she's done to help me out.

Until we get back Home and scan our lives, we won't be able to fully grasp just how much our guides were on our side and even minimized trauma. They're truly always trying to help us fulfill our charts, and most don't get any credit for it . . . which makes what they do a genuine act of love.

(If you'd like to reach the Temple of Spirit Guides through meditation, please turn to page 237 after reading the instructions on pages 181–184.)

(If you'd like to reach the Temple of Spirit Guides through meditation, please turn to page 237 after reading the instructions on pages 181–184.)

🏵 🏵 🏵

PART III

Halls That Can Truly Help Us on Earth

Chapter 19

THE HALL
OF CHARTS

The Hall of Charts is made of pink marble with only two (yet gigantic) columns at its main entrance. It's not an enclosed building, but is instead open on all sides so that people can come and go easily. Under its roof you'll find a large space with lots of seats, along with a spectacular waterfall just inside the main entrance; the water runs from the falls into a great fountain that changes colors.

The building sits back a little from the other temples and is surrounded by lovely trees of every variation. There are no formal gardens, so the landscape forms a natural-wildlife type of refuge. This is where various animals such as deer, squirrels, gazelles, raccoons, and chipmunks tend to be found, meandering about the grounds. It is very beautiful and calming here, as the Hall of Charts exudes the beauty of nature.

Now while all of the temples on the Other Side are very important, this particular one is crucial for outgoing souls because this is where individuals' charts are planned. It can also be a great help to those of us still in life, for we can view our souls' progression. Please note, however, that this chapter is somewhat different in that I'm going to spend it detailing charts themselves, not this particular temple. The meditation on page 241 will help you reach the Hall of Charts to receive its aid.

Making a Chart and Going to School

Francine says that creating a chart is a very intricate process that is considered to be time-consuming even on the Other Side, and it's one of the most important things we do because it has so many facets to it. We want to advance our souls, so successful charts need to include all the different emotions or experiences that life has to offer. These include the accidents, joys, passions, fears, and a million other things—whatever we can possibly think of can be put in so that we can learn. Francine says that from the very moment we started on this reincarnation schematic, we picked a certain number of lives, the time we'd spend in each, and what lessons we'd have to learn for God and our own souls . . . and when that's all done, we go Home.

One of the most useful—and most used—tools for our learning process is reincarnation. It simply isn't logical to think that we only live one life, especially when a child dies or we see that some are born into abject poverty and others into incredible wealth. Reincarnation not only explains these seeming inequities of life, but even more important, it helps us understand things on a larger scale.

After coming Home and going through orientation, we decide whether or not we're going to experience another life on Earth. We don't do this to atone for anything or for our own karma, but rather to gain some more knowledge to help us perfect. (We could even say that karma is actually the realization of our souls.) If we thought we were too harsh or unfair in one life, for instance, we could choose to experience some rejection in our next one; or if we were too introverted, we'd pick a more outgoing incarnation the next time. As hard as it may be to understand, we could even decide to go through trauma or take an early exit—not because we're dark souls, but so we can experience everything.

As I've said many times, total or complete knowledge has to include experience. Although you can read about things in a book, unless you've actually gone through them yourself, you'll never truly get the intellectual and especially emotional impact that they bring. For example, if someone breaks a leg, you can have empathy and sympathy because you know that he or she is in pain, but if you've never suffered that injury yourself, your reaction won't be as strong as that of someone who has. In other words, it's impossible to relate to pain unless you actually go through it.

Think about the plight of poverty-stricken and starving children in various parts of the world, which results in different reactions from different people: Some will see them and basically have no emotional response whatsoever; others will say, "Oh my God, look at those poor children," and feel bad until something else grabs their attention a few minutes later; and still others will actually act on their distress by sending in a donation or joining an organization that helps these kids. Of course there are many other reactions besides the ones I've mentioned, but I think you can see that people's experiences and makeup determine their emotional and intellectual responses to any given situation.

Using the illustration above, the first person probably isn't very spiritual or sympathetic and hasn't had that much experience in living lives. The second seems fairly spiritual outwardly, but it's not necessarily to the point where it's a mainstay of his or her life. And the final individual, who's likely on his or her last life, is very spiritual in nature and uses that wisdom on a daily basis. I know I'm oversimplifying in this example because there are many good, caring, pious people out there who aren't running off to join the Peace Corps; my point here is that all of us have varying degrees of experiential knowledge, so we consequently have varying degrees of spirituality. You may wonder why that is, or perhaps you're posing the questions that humankind has asked since the very beginning of time: "Why am I here?" and "What is the purpose of life?"

Well, the purpose of life is fairly simple—to learn and gain knowledge for our own soul's perfection and for Mother and Father God. Some of you might be asking, "Why are we gaining knowledge for our Creators? Don't They know everything?" Yes, They do, but you must remember that every one of us is a part of Them. Each individual soul is unique and important, and as I like to put it, a "miniature God." We all have little pieces of knowledge that come together to make the complete picture, as it were. So it's as if we're each a sliver of a giant pie, and without our small sections, the pie can't be whole. All of our Parents' creations come together to make up total experiential knowledge in Their now.

Now since everything in nature has a counterpart or another half, so it is with God: Our Father holds us together with intellect and His controlling energy, whereas our Mother is the miracle worker who takes a more hands-on approach. And since the heavenly, perfect environment of the Other Side has no negativity or evil, They send us into life on Earth to test our intellectual and emotional makeup. This hellish planet gives us a true perspective on what's good and positive.

As much as the book of Genesis is an allegory, it's also very truthful in the sense that the only way Adam and Eve, who represented humankind, could gain *all* knowledge was to leave the place where no evil existed and go where it did. Thus the chart came into being—so we humans could be shielded from the damage of this dark world while we perfected.

I've always said that the Earth plane is nothing more than a school for learning about evil and negativity . . . it's as simple as that. Just like college, life on this planet is a temporary experience, and you have many subjects to study and learn from. You see your counselors (Council members and your spirit guide) before you start school and map out your curriculum (your chart) so that you can gain knowledge in the most efficient and quick way possible, and you choose your major (your main life themes) and your minor (your option line or subthemes).

You then go to the classes you've chosen (following your chart) and learn what each of them has to offer (living on Earth). If you don't pass a course, you may have to take it again, or you might choose some electives to augment your overall education (reincarnation), but you'll eventually graduate with a bachelor's degree, a master's, or a Ph.D. (depending upon your free-will choice of what level you want to evolve your soul) and go into the real world (the Other Side) with your head held high. You'll live for eternity fortified by everything you've learned.

We try to get as much assistance as we can while we're writing our charts, consulting with the Council, the person who has agreed to be our spirit guide, and a special phylum of angels called "the Virtues." (I'll talk about them more later in the chapter.)

I cannot stress enough how much the Council helps us during this process, advising us if we're going too fast, or letting us know that we've had too recent of a life and aren't prepared to go into another right away. They may also say that we can get through our charts in a shorter time because we have more strength than we think we do, or that we must be careful because we've taken on too much and are fragile.

But here's where the rub comes in: We have full free-will choice on the Other Side and are in a perfect state over there. It's like accepting an invitation to do something on a day when we feel great, only to find that when the actual date comes around we don't feel well and wish we could get out of our obligation. In our bliss at Home, we choose what we want in our chart, not fully realizing that we won't have that strength on the Earth plane.

In fact, what we call "bleed-throughs" often follow us from life to life through phobias, fears, or even certain illnesses that we died from or were crippled by. Francine says that although the Council tries to warn us about past-life experiences bleeding through, when we incarnate we go ahead and carry our memories in our subconscious, which then get absorbed by the cells in our bodies. Therefore, if we had a heart condition in a past life, its memory can get absorbed into the cells around the heart in *this* life, thus continuing the old problem.

We may also disagree with the Council and take on too much because, after all, they don't order us around; we always have the final say as far as our charts are concerned. I'm sure that when times get tough down here, we wonder, *What was wrong with me when I made my chart?* or even worse, *Why didn't I listen?* Yet when we get back Home, Council members will never say "I told you so," for they know that this is part of our learning, too.

Most of us misunderstand the concept of free will, which is confined to the Other Side. So when we make up our charts, we freely choose what we want to accomplish and experience in life;

however, once we've completed them and "signed our contracts" by incarnating, we can't break them. All charts have options or tests inside of them, which we choose to deliberately include to measure our spirituality and the overall progression of our soul. This is where things can become confusing, as it seems that we make choices using free will on Earth, but we're actually just listening to our own souls or the "God within," which can manifest in several ways.

Your own God within can be heard via your conscience or your innate sense that something's right or wrong. This feeling is part of your soul's experience and knowledge, and it means that your soul is trying to communicate with you. If you're evolved enough to listen, then things will most likely turn out for the better. If you ignore these messages, on the other hand, life can get more difficult. It's important to keep in mind that people who don't listen to their own souls will find themselves going off track on their chart more than those who do listen.

The consequences of going off track mean that we'll probably have to go through another existence or two to get it right. Naturally we all want to succeed, and most of us do—but again, just like school, we have fast and slow learners. So some of us follow our charts and quickly attain what we want for ourselves, while others may have a more difficult time following our charts, so our evolution is more gradual. But our Creators are loving and merciful and allow such "slow learners" all of the time and lives necessary to eventually acquire knowledge and evolve.

Choices and Challenges

Francine says that none of us could have any idea of how intricate and precise our charts have to be, which is why we need so much advising in the process. A chart must cover every single nuance and facet of the experiences we'll encounter in life, including our times of birth and death (with details on how we'll die); our family members, friends, and loves; our marriage(s) or lack thereof; our children, if any; our griefs, losses, gains, so-called accidents, illnesses, and joys; where we live and when we move; our physical appearance and handicaps, if any; our gender, race, and ethnic background; our religion, if any; our level of education; our socioeconomic status; and on and on it goes.

A chart is so specific that we have to meet with all of the individuals who will have any significant effect on our lives, which is done in a huge meeting room in the Hall of Charts. Here we'll encounter numerous people, including our family members, friends, and acquaintances, along with total strangers. Anyone who has any kind of an impact on our lives will be in that room to go over our charts and see where they fit in—their charts have to intertwine with ours in such a way that we can all learn. These individuals may be involved in small incidents that help us with big lessons, or they could be part of traumatic episodes that cause us some harm or grief . . . it all depends on what we choose to learn and how we want to learn it.

Each chart must also take global and local events into consideration, as well as private and personal occurrences that could impact our charts and make them go in a completely different direction. These option lines are built into each chart to give us some flexibility in taking several roads to the same destination, so to speak, by learning even more than we originally intended.

Francine says that because charts must contain everything from the smallest of details to the most earth-shattering of catastrophes—from the total stranger who does something so kind that you remember it forever to a hurricane that destroys your home—she can't even begin to describe how much effort and precise planning is necessary. So when clients ask me, "You mean I *chose* to go through this nightmare in my life?" I always have to truthfully answer, "Yes, you did. Every single thing in your chart is tracked, and nothing is left to chance."

Some charts contain traumatic events so that individuals can learn about loss or experience grief, such as in the death of a child. Souls who write this type of incident into their lives are counseled heavily by the Council as to whether or not they can handle it. We must also remember that those who have experienced such events also received an agreement from the entity who died to do so early.

You see, incarnations are not only for souls' own learning experience, but also to help others gain wisdom as well. When you think about it, the intertwining of lives can be wonderful or tragic, but it's very intricately planned and always has a purpose, whether it's to give assistance or to be part of a lesson that has to be learned. Yes, we all suffer and grieve when we lose loved ones, especially if we feel that they died too early, but we must take solace in the fact that we all chose every experience and will be together on the Other Side very soon.

If you've had a hard or tragic life, please don't ever feel that you're a bad person who's paying for something from a past incarnation. If you were, you wouldn't have even picked up this book; those by authors such as Wayne Dyer, Deepak Chopra, Caroline Myss, and other spiritual writers; or the Bible, because you wouldn't care.

Dark entities never wonder if they're on track because they simply justify all their actions—and what's even more aggravating is that they never seem to have any remorse. Good people, on the other hand, feel guilty about things they didn't mean to do or that they inadvertently did, placing a great deal of blame on themselves.

Now as a white entity, you can choose to elongate incidents in your life or shorten them. You even choose your exit points (times when you can decide to leave life early and go to the Other Side because you've accomplished what you wanted to in this incarnation). All charts have five exit points, which usually take the form of a near-death accident or a scenario in which one could die, such as contracting a sudden illness. Many souls bypass the exit points and continue following their charts, while others take a particular exit point because they feel that they've learned enough.

I've very rarely seen anyone go "before their time," even though it can seem that way to us because we can't read anyone's chart here. And interestingly enough, I've found that people who are spiritually on track, or those who at least try to stay on track and are constantly concerned about whether they are, actually have easier exits. I think it's because they know where they're going.

Now I'm not suggesting here that we should end our own lives, because suicide is *never* the answer. In the larger picture, such deaths occur because the souls in question picked lives that were more than they could handle. Of course when they were writing their charts in the perfect environment of the Other Side, they probably felt that they could handle anything. The Council invariably warned them about taking on too much, or they advised the individuals to tone down some areas so that they'd have better chances for success. While most do take the Elders' suggestions, others feel that they know better, so they charge on ahead and don't change their charts . . . making them prime candidates for committing suicide.

This act is considered a great sin in most religions, especially Christianity, which believes that individuals who kill themselves are damned to hell forever. Francine confirms that there's no fiery pit inhabited with demons that torture humans who have "sinned" for all eternity, for our Creators would never have allowed such a place to be created in the first place. Remember, They don't have emotions such as malice, hatefulness, or vengeance . . . these feelings are strictly human. And as the Earth plane is the only place where evil and negativity exist, it's the only hell there is.

It's also important to note that not all self-inflicted deaths can be classified as suicides. For example, those who accidentally take too many drugs or mix them together in a lethal dose, or those who kill themselves because of a mental illness such as schizophrenia, deep depression, or bipolar disorder aren't considered to be genuine suicides on the Other Side. The individuals must have a true motive to end things—when it's done out of spite, or because they're tired of life or want to escape their responsibilities, then *that's* considered a suicide. Such people have to come right back and live the same type of existence all over again. This isn't a punishment, for they're just being sent back to complete their charts, which they'd already chosen to do. All souls spend a great amount of effort making their charts, so suicide makes that initial effort to live it fruitless. Personally, I can think of no greater deterrent to committing suicide than to know that I'd just have to go through the same type of life all over again.

Getting back to our charts, we also get help with them from the Virtues, a phylum of angels that helps escort souls into and out of life.

Just before we incarnate, we say our good-byes to our friends and loved ones on the Other Side and give one last thumbs-up to the person who is to be our spirit guide. We then go into seclusion for a short time to gather our thoughts and meditate on our upcoming existence, and here's where the Virtues come into play. It seems that these angels have a special communication with our Creators and also serve as sentinels and escorts for outgoing and incoming souls.

One of the first entities you will meet upon passing will probably be a Virtue to help you over to the Other Side, and this is most likely the last one you'll see before you incarnate. Virtues don't assist you in planning your chart as the Council and your guide do, but they help you go over it one last time in contemplative seclusion. They also have the power to alter your chart without getting permission from the Council. Whether they've been infused by God or not, they have complete knowledge of your chart, so they'll ask you questions and make suggestions that may cause some last-minute alterations. Once you're satisfied that your chart is finalized and complete, you're then helped into the womb of your life mother by the Virtue. (For more on the Virtues, please see my *Book of Angels*.)

Most entities don't enter their mother's womb until about the seventh or eighth month of pregnancy (unless they know that they're going to be born prematurely). There's no need to enter earlier, and those who do usually get bored and never do it again. As souls enter into the bodies of the babies-to-be, their conscious mental acuity starts to lessen, and all knowledge becomes ensconced in the subconscious. Almost all conscious memory has faded away by the time they're born.

What's fascinating, however, is that many young children being born today are carrying those memories with them and are seeming to speak about them more frequently. For example, a woman told me that one day out of the blue, her three-and-a-half-year-old son started to talk about his real Home, where he said he'd come from. This mother was very smart and listened closely to her toddler, inquiring, "What does it look like?"

He replied, "It's beautiful, with many shining buildings with big round sticks [columns]. They have flowers and gardens, and we all talk and laugh and play."

She asked, "Are there animals?"

She said that he looked at her as if she were stupid and answered, "You remember, Mama, it's full of all kinds of animals." He then said, "There is also a beautiful woman who stands in roses." [This sounds like the breathtaking statue of Azna in the famous rose gardens of the Other Side.]

"This place must be very far up," the mother remarked.

"No, silly," he responded, "it's right here." And she swore that she almost fell over when his hand measured about his own height of three feet off of our ground level. She told me she was in awe because she'd just read a book of mine in which I explained that the Other Side is indeed about three feet above the Earth plane. She hadn't discussed this book with anyone, and of course her son couldn't read yet. As she concluded her story, I just smiled, for this is what gives my work validity and inspires me to keep on researching.

All My Lives and Friends

As souls evolve, they usually choose to write more difficult and intricate charts to gain as much knowledge as possible, whereas entities who are incarnating for the first time will have a fairly simple chart written (that is, in comparison to others, for no life is easy). People often ask me what the average number of lives is, but there isn't any. Some individuals will finish what they feel is their goal of perfection in 20 to 30 lives, while others will take on more. However, in more than 50 years of doing readings, I've never encountered anyone who was on his or her first incarnation and have rarely found anyone living more than 100 times.

Many people think that the more a soul incarnates, the more advanced it is, and that's just not true. The evolvement of the soul depends on the *type* of existence chosen, not the number, so a person who decides to have ten fairly simple and uneventful lives may not gain as much knowledge and experience as someone who picks one filled with interaction, trauma, and many challenges. For example, Francine only lived one life, which was quite traumatic because she lost a daughter and was herself killed by Spanish conquistadors. Thus, she chose to perfect by being my guide. (Boy, was she in for a surprise!)

My spirit guide is a very evolved soul who has actually had many existences on other planets, and she's related to me more than once that Earth is much too barbaric for her to come into life here again. So when she told me that I'd gone around on this planet 54 times, I asked her what in God's name was wrong with me . . . why couldn't I learn? She said that didn't have anything to do with it, for many of my lives were short, and I took on some extra ones because I wanted to gain knowledge for God.

Francine also said that people once died at a much younger age, so they were able to take on more lives. We humans used to expire at age 40 but are now easily living to be 80, so most of us are getting two time lines of life in one. In fact, my good friend Zahi Hawass (who is the secretary-general of the Egyptian Supreme Council of Antiquities), told me that he's found many mummies who died in their teens from abscessed teeth, of all things. It seems that several tons of sand used to fall on Cairo every day, so people ate sand with their food and greatly wore their teeth down, and of course there weren't any dentists to help out. And with life spans so short in earlier times, it's no wonder that people in Egypt—as well as India, Persia, and the Orient—got married at the age of ten.

Now while our spirit guides help us with our charts and lives, let's just say that my situation is a little unusual. Because I came into this life as a psychic and a trance medium, Francine had to learn how to enter my body while I exited it, as well as how to breathe, work my organs, and use my vocal cords. Even though there's no time on the Other Side, she calculated that she studied to be my guide for about what would equal 700 years in our time.

Of course that sounds like a lot to us, and is even extensive to those at Home, but she has assured me that by no means did it feel like 700 years to her.

One usually has a different spirit guide for every life, and this is the first time that Francine has been mine. So you may wonder how she knew that she was going to be my guide so far in advance of when I actually incarnated. Well, she says that all of us have what we might call a "master chart," which takes into consideration how much spirituality we want to attain, including how many lives and what types of incarnations we want to have in order to obtain that goal. It's essentially our master plan for gaining spirituality through the reincarnation schematic, which is then broken down into individual life charts. Thus, Francine and I planned for her to be my guide, as well as what this life I'd chosen for myself would be like. So I actually had five or six existences while she was busy studying and preparing to be my guide in this incarnation.

All spirit guides have to learn to become somewhat more humanized or attuned to the way we react and use our emotions on the Earth plane. If they didn't, they wouldn't necessarily care about our concerns because they'd just feel that everything would be over soon and we'd be back on the Other Side. I guess you could say that they have to learn to have more empathy for the plight of their charges. Even now if I ask Francine something, I often get her famous line: "Everything will be all right." I've screamed back, "What does *that* mean?! I could die and everything will be all right?!"

All guides can give help and communicate—while they don't necessarily do so through voice contact (like I get from Francine), they all send us messages through our minds. We think that we suddenly thought to call Susan out of the blue and see how she's doing, for example, but that's our guides at work. They send us many messages, solutions, and aid over the course of each day, which we chalk up to coincidence or our own deductive reasoning.

Of course we do bypass our guides at times to get the infusions in our own psychic ability or intellect. Francine never helps me with my readings, for instance—I know that my ability comes directly from God. Now if you come to a trance as even my dear friend Montel Williams has, Francine is a wealth of information. His experience with her made such an impression that he told a group of about 200 people before a taping that it was the most spiritual and amazing thing he'd ever seen. He even went on to effusively recount that she knew details about him and his family that no one else could possibly know. To this day, he says it was a life-changing experience.

While we're on the subject of Montel, if you look at the back of some of my books, there's a quote from him that says he doesn't believe in psychics but believes in me. Well, I love him with all my heart, and the world can't even begin to know how much he does for others in need. For the entire 16 years I've been appearing on his show, we've never made a written contract; one simple exchange has kept us together for so long. He asked, "Girlfriend [his nickname for me], will you just stay with me?" and I replied, "You got it." From that day on, it has only been a friendship and loyalty contract, bound by my word and his. I'm so lucky to have him as a friend; and we've stood by each other through sickness, divorce, and all of life's problems.

The other day he said, "I've always got your back." You're going to read it here first: I have *his* back, too. I would do anything that I could for him, including, as he says, "moving a mountain." You don't find this kind of friendship and pure love in life that often . . . and when you do, you bless it.

I had to get that in print for myself and posterity, yet I have so many good friends whom I love dearly, as I do all of my readers and fans. I greatly appreciate the compassion, generosity, and support that you've always given me. (Yes, I'm having a little emotional interlude here, but as the writer, I feel that's my privilege.)

Chapter 20

THE TEMPLE
OF PENANCE

The Temple of Penance is a Romanesque building that's set back a little from the other halls and is much smaller than they are. Francine says that not everyone wants or needs to go here, but entities on their last lives especially want to, and it can be a great help for those of us still on Earth.

Now when I first heard about this hall, I have to tell you that I was put off. Having been raised in a Lutheran, Catholic, Episcopalian, and Jewish home, the word *penance* is not a pleasant one for me, as it conjures up praying or sacrificing to atone for some supposed sin or wrongdoing. And most religions define it as making restitution through prayers, acts of kindness, and even the use of "corporal mortification."

Happily, this hall has nothing to do with all that—it doesn't exist to punish us or show us what we've done wrong or whether we'll live another life or not. We do view events of our lives on another scanner, but this time we're focusing on unfinished business or missed opportunities. Perhaps we were unable to tell someone good-bye, or we treated another person poorly and never got a chance to explain or make amends. This is basically the place where we tie up all the loose ends of what might be on our conscience.

Those who have completed their last lives go to this temple regularly, for it's like a cleansing process to eliminate any carried-over concerns about actions and relationships that they've had in all their incarnations. It's a baptism of sorts, which allows them to live forever on the Other Side free from any pangs of conscience that they might have had. And those of us still on Earth can use the opportunity to visit this hall and take care of anything that's bothering us now, before we even get back Home.

With our charts in hand, we can meet with any person we wish to call upon in the Temple of Penance, with the specific purpose of working out any confusion or animosity. Sometimes living on this planet can cause us to take a different road to the same destination, which doesn't necessarily mean that we've gone off track. We've just said or done things we didn't mean, such as being excessively rude or hurting someone's feelings. So after our charts are reviewed in the Halls of Wisdom and Justice, we can make amends for infractions by word or deed to those we have possibly harmed . . . we just want to make it right, and the Temple of Penance exists for us to do so.

After Francine mentioned this hall in our salon, I got a very interesting letter from a man who'd gone home and reached the Temple of Penance during a meditation. He saw himself during the time of the great potato famine in Ireland, and his family was starving because all the crops were dying from a funguslike disease. As he was walking along a road that headed toward his farm, he was in agony because he had nothing to take home to his hungry wife and children. Then he spotted two chickens that had wandered close to a fence, which belonged to a neighboring farmer.

Since the two were friends, this man was aware that these chickens were all the farmer had left for food, but he nonetheless stole one of them out of desperation. He took it home and cooked it for his grateful family, and didn't feel bad about what he'd done. Yet as he viewed the incident now, he was able to see the effects his actions had on his neighbor (remember that all charts are intertwined and we can view it all on the Other Side). My client felt bad because his family had made it to America in that life, but the other farmer hadn't. He knew it wasn't just because he took the chicken, but he still wanted to meet his neighbor and make it right.

My client met his former friend in the Temple of Penance and was immediately relieved when his neighbor told him that he knew all about the incident from viewing his own chart. My client apologized, saying that he now understood that he'd had a pure motive to steal in order to feed his starving family, and that under ordinary circumstances he never would have done anything like this. The two men then reminisced for a while and ultimately parted on very good terms.

Coming Home from a human life, almost all of us have a sense that loose ends must be tied up. If we feel bad about what we did to others, chances are that they really paid no mind to it or just chalked it up as a learning process. This is due, of course, to the fact that when the offended parties pass over, they review their own charts, and because of the mind coming to full acuity, they understand more completely why certain things occur. This is what happened with the offended farmer in the above story, who came to realize that the theft of the chicken was perpetrated to feed a starving family.

I find it interesting that after the reincarnation schematic is over, this hall will no longer be needed. It does serve as good therapy, though, and it seems that the most sensitive entities are the ones you'll tend to find here.

You see, we're the best of ourselves that we can be on the Other Side—we're ultimately more spiritual and elevated, but we don't lose our core personality or basic self, which I've always thought was wonderful. The best of us stays, but the false or protective overlays of behavior that served us on Earth fall away and reveal our true self. It's nice to know that this site exists in order to rid ourselves of any remaining earthly negativity or concerns, leaving us to fully enjoy ourselves at Home.

(If you'd like to reach the Temple of Penance through meditation, please turn to page 245 after reading the instructions on pages 181–184.)

Chapter 21

THE HALL OF RECONNECTION

The Hall of Reconnection is Romanesque in design, with many golden columns and a foyer that leads to two huge brass doors. However, Francine says that it's really only usable and functional for those of us on the Earth plane to make a connection with a dead loved one. (Of course on the Other Side, they call *us* the dead and consider themselves the living. When you think about it, it makes sense because this life is so brief and transient, while our Home is eternal.)

In fact, when the reincarnation schematic is over and everyone has learned from their charts, the Hall of Reconnection will be dissolved, along with the Temple of Penance. They won't be needed anymore because all of us will have completed our missions and will be together on the Other Side. Then we won't have to connect with anyone because everyone we have ever loved will be over there with us.

You can visit the Hall of Reconnection by using the meditation on page 247 or by asking before sleep to have your guide as well as your angels take you there. Yet this time you'll be entering the building alone. Your guide and angels aren't ignoring you here; they're just giving you some privacy so that you won't feel self-conscious when meeting the soul you want to reconnect with.

Entering this temple is an extremely powerful experience. Many people who see loved ones in so-called dreams or in an astral state have actually gone here, whether they realize it or not. So if you don't get to this hall right away, don't give up—keep trying every night for at least a week. I'm told that the Council says nine attempts in a row is more of a surety that you'll get there, for nine has always been a spiritual number. (I'm convinced that's because it's a triple trinity number.) Much like when someone tells you that they just ate at the most fabulous restaurant in the world but you don't know where it is, when you finally get to the Hall of Reconnection, it will be incredibly rewarding for you.

You will indeed see your passed-over loved ones in all their glory, but you have to realize that they will appear to be 30 years old. In one of his books, Robert Monroe tells a fascinating story of visiting the Other Side through astral projection. A nice young man smiled and waved at him, and Monroe waved back but then promptly forgot the incident. Later he was told by his guide that the waving man was actually his father at age 30. When Monroe went over again, he wasn't so noncommittal and had a nice talk with his dad.

As Francine says, "There have been many times when I have seen people walk right by their family members without knowing who they were. Sometimes children don't know or can't remember what their parents or grandparents looked like at that age, but please keep this in mind because it is so important: This ignorance only happens in the meditative, astral, or regressive states. Souls recognize each other immediately when they pass over and go Home."

My spirit guide emphasizes that you must call your loved ones' names in this hall; or before you go into an altered state, ask them to walk up to you and identify themselves. There are times when they'll assume the visages you remember, but most choose to peel off the years and not keep the old mantle on when they go down the tunnel. Interestingly, even now when I dream about my father, who has been gone 11 years at the time of this writing (it's hard to believe it's been that long!), each time he looks healthier, younger, and more vital. He died at the age of 88, but now he looks about 50. I'm sure that as I keep dreaming, he'll get younger and younger until he reaches 30.

So don't be surprised if someone comes up to you and says that he or she is John, Maria, or Peter and was your child, aunt, or parent. Acknowledge that person, for in a few minutes you'll realize that he or she is indeed that individual. Of course no words are exchanged, for you'll do what Francine calls "mind talk." This is a very sophisticated form of telepathy, which does not just comprise mental impressions, but actual formulated words.

A Question-and-Answer Session with Francine

When Francine first shared information about this temple in our salon, it sparked so many questions that I decided to include most of them right here, along with her answers. While a few of the queries may seem personal in nature, I believe that we can all gain something from them.

Q. *"How quickly do children on your side reach age 30?"*

A. "As soon as they go down the tunnel—it's the same for everyone, whether they're old, newborn, or middle-aged. Please be aware, though, that in the case of babies who are stillborn, miscarried, or born but then die shortly thereafter, entities don't ever actually come in. We don't feel that these are real charts, for the only thing that these situations do is help the parents and family grow or learn spiritually. Sylvia had seven miscarriages—four before Paul, and three after Christopher—but no souls ever came in. However, when he was about three, Paul did tell Sylvia, 'Mom, it sure took me a long time to get here.'"

Q. "When can we go to the Hall of Reconnection?"

A. "You can do it anytime during sleep or meditation, regardless of the time of day. For some of you who are busy, it's often easier to try the practice at night; but even if you can carve out 10 or 15 minutes for this pursuit, you'll be surprised at how proficient you get at it, particularly because time is different on our side."

Q. "Should we have a white candle burning when we do this?"

A. "You don't have to. If I were living a life like you, I would ask any of my loved ones or ancestors or just anyone who wanted to reconnect with me to come over and tell me their name and relationship and then give me any information they had."

Q. "Could we ask for Council members to help us in this temple?"

A. "Yes, anyone and everyone is available, even those whom you might deem to be famous figures, such as Albert Einstein, Abraham Lincoln, or Martin Luther King—anyone who is available will come. Remember that we know everyone over here, although I understand how hard it is for your finite minds to comprehend this."

Q. "If we're trying to clear out pain or some of these negative patterns in our lives, can we go back and forth to these halls?"

A. "That's an excellent question. Yes, you can—and from what I've seen, it's what really works the best. So if you have some sort of pain or addiction, go to the Hall of Remembrance and find out the root of where, when, or in what life it started; then go to the Hall of Healing with this information because you're now armed with the beginning of the problem. Please state (and mean) that you know it was charted and that you learned from it, and now you want it uprooted and healed.

"You can go back and forth as many times as you want for the same thing or for different maladies, worries, or phobias. You will be enlightened because knowledge is power, but it also sets you free. It really doesn't matter which temple you go to first, for if you should be at one rather than another, Council members, your guide, or angels will guide you there to get the best results. We all know your chart from the Hall of Records, so we know what you need . . . sometimes better than you do. However, we can only recommend—we don't force you."

Q. *"Can we take dark entities into any of the halls?"*

A. "Absolutely not! God wouldn't let them in, or even through the tunnel—when they die, they go right back in utero. But remember that at the end of Earth's schematic of reincarnation, our Father will absorb them back into His uncreated mass. You all, on the other hand, will always keep your identity and live on the Other Side."

Q. *"If I go to the Hall of Reconnection, will I be able to talk to my father and find out why he had such a hard life and had to go through so much?"*

A. "I realize that this will be hard for you to understand, but I know your father and he was a good man in life, but he was also very stubborn and closed off. He is telling me to say to you now, 'I wrote this and this is the way I wanted it to go. You see, the vision you have of what I should have done or how I should have lived my life has no bearing on what my soul had recorded to perfect for God. You are only looking at it from your own feelings of righteousness or justice. I knew I was good, but my suffering only perfected me more for God.'

"He goes on to say, 'While we are all linked, our chart and contracts with ourselves and God are very personal and often secret.' So he wouldn't have changed anything; and while he appreciates your concern, you're not seeing the big picture.

"You can't interfere with others' charts. You can comfort the individuals, but remember that they contracted to go through everything in their lives. So you shouldn't get caught in that endless cycle of 'Why do good people suffer?' Good people are the only ones who want to perfect; dark-souled entities don't care. You may think something is 'unfair' from where you are in life because you're seeing though a narrow beam of light—you don't see the whole beauty of the room, so to speak. You can't tell those who wrote it that it's unfair because they chose to go through this and have their soul grow from a hard life."

About four months after this trance with Francine was over, I got a letter from an attendee who was doing a definitive genealogy of her family and had been stuck for eight years on her father's side. She'd gotten as far as a great-great-grandfather named Jacob but couldn't trace his family, particularly his wife.

This had her stumped, so she tried the Hall of Reconnection. After four attempts she found herself in this beautiful temple, and a lovely woman with a white dress and a Gibson-girl hairdo approached her. She stated that her name was Emma Crawford and she'd been born in England; had married Jacob but died in childbirth; and was buried in Tulsa, Oklahoma. My client checked this lead out when she awoke, and sure enough, she tracked down Emma. From there she was able to pick up the missing trail, and she continued her search without any further problems. I think this shows that there's no reason too small or frivolous to go to the Hall of Reconnection.

Seeing your loved ones will be of great solace, but don't be afraid to validate someone you don't recognize—even to the point that it's something you don't know and have to research later. You don't know how many times I've called out a name or situation to people in a reading or at a lecture, and while they didn't make the connection at the time, they've called me later and confirmed that it was Aunt So-and-So, whom the person didn't know but another family member had remembered very well.

I also heard from a woman who'd attended the trance with Francine. This particular attendee had lost her son at the age of 21, and no matter how hard she tried, she couldn't get any reciprocation from him—visual or otherwise. Before my guide came in, I'd described the khaki jacket this woman's son was wearing when he died, his baseball-card collection, the slight limp in his left leg, and other similar things. She was in tears upon getting this validation but was so bereaved that she said, "I just want to see him one more time because I didn't get to say good-bye." So she decided that she'd try to contact her boy through the Hall of Reconnection.

After her fifth or sixth attempt, she was finally successful and walked through the temple's doors to see her son, just as she remembered him. He sat with her on a marble bench and explained that he'd had 51 lives, and it had simply been his time to go. He assured her that he knew her grief was very real but that they'd be together soon. He also told her about some future events, such as that she'd enroll in school and do therapy work (which she'd never previously considered). Before she left, he put something in her hand and closed her fingers over it.

My client awoke with a start and felt a little skeptical about what had happened, until she noticed her closed hand. When she opened it, she almost fainted . . . there sat a small gold band with a crisscross pattern, which her son had always worn on his pinkie and had been buried with. Not long after this, she also had the opportunity to enter a psychology program for grieving parents.

No, not everyone who visits the Hall of Reconnection will come back with a tangible object from their loved ones, but you'd be surprised by how many times they send us necklaces, rings, notes, feathers, coins, flowers, and the like. Such things tend to show up if we're just aware of the out of the ordinary and don't dismiss it as "coincidence."

Passed-over loved ones can also leave scents, make popping noises, play music, ring phones, make lights blink on and off, move objects, and even touch us, among other things. For instance, as I mentioned earlier in the book, "Somewhere Over the Rainbow" was my father's song for me, and whenever I feel down, it seems to find me. Even when I was driving to my office right after he died, it came on the radio—now this was certainly no longer a popular tune at the time, so for it to appear at that moment was a clear sign from him.

Another time I was so worried about finances that I almost made myself sick. I'd just moved into a small apartment, and I was sitting in my bedroom trying to unpack. I pulled a beige telephone out of one of the boxes and set it on the floor, and a couple of minutes later, it began to ring. The cord was lying naked on the floor because I hadn't plugged it in anywhere yet, and here the phone was ringing. After staring at it for a few moments, I picked it up. As plain as day, I heard my dad's voice say, "It's all okay."

Although I've been in this work all my life, nothing like that had ever happened to me before. But since I'm also a researcher, I traced the cord again . . . sure enough, it was just a dead phone lying there, not connected to anything. I even went so far as to ask two different installers if a telephone could ring on its own without being in the wall connection. They both looked at me as if I had a screw loose, and one of them replied, "Ma'am, the ringer doesn't work until we connect the telephone line to the outlet— even if it's plugged in." So there you have it. Even *I* have to validate everything, otherwise I might go the other way and get too "airy fairy" and start seeing unicorns and elves that talk . . . and then obsessively smudge my house until everyone is sick.

If we just keep things practical, simple, and logical, God will show us that the veil between this dimension and the Other Side is thinning to the point that it's almost gossamer.

Chapter 22

THE HALL
OF HEALING

The Hall of Healing is one of the most important buildings I'm discussing in this book because we now live in a world with so much mental and physical distress. Obviously, those on the Other Side don't need any healing because there's no illness over there. Those who pass through the tunnel at death not only go back to the age of 30, but their bodies and minds become whole as well. If they were crippled, had lost limbs, suffered from injuries or pain, or had mental illness in life, their bodies and minds quickly return to the perfection of the Other Side. All physical injuries disappear, all pain evaporates, and bodies and minds feel so great that it defies description. They have unlimited energy, nothing hurts anywhere, and their brains are at full capacity.

As my grandmother used to say, there are few times in life when we don't experience some of its pinpricks. We're either tired mentally or physically; have a headache or a pulled muscle; or suffer from diabetes, heart disease, back problems, and on and on it goes. None of these ailments exist on the Other Side . . . not a single one. Therefore, we can only assume that the Hall of Healing is for those of us still in life, not for anybody on the Other Side.

Francine says that this building is probably the most stunning of all the Romanesque temples of our Home, with large pillars at the front and a huge glass dome on the roof that projects a beautiful and healing green light to the entire interior of the hall. And then there's the statue of the Mother God, glowing ebony with green eyes, on a pedestal in the center of the building. She has a very voluptuous figure and wears golden armor and carries a sword. (It reminds me of the stereotypical image of an opera singer, but without the hat and horns of a Viking.) The sword is not intended for violent purposes, but rather to symbolize that She can cut through negativity. Remember that the sword makes a cross—which is why I tell people to mentally put a golden sword in front of them when they meditate, going across their forehead and extending down to their pelvis area to deflect negativity. This statue is unique in that it can change form and Azna can come down off the pedestal to embrace you and even speak to you.

Much like the Temple of Azna (which I'll discuss in the next chapter), the Hall of Healing has a great presence of the Mother God, Who is the miracle worker for all of us in life. Along with our Home, the Earth plane is Her dominion because She is the Activator Who performs miracles and is the only one Who can change or manipulate a person's chart. Although She has many statues and shrines dedicated to Her on the Other Side and intermingles frequently with entities there, the Hall of Healing finds Her healing energy manifesting when Her statue comes to life. I don't know why, but I'm convinced that when that stone figure comes alive, a miracle occurs—maybe not an overt miracle in all cases, but certainly one that brings sustenance and relief to the soul.

Francine says that inside the Hall of Healing are many golden-glass cubicles shaped like pyramids, and you're encouraged by attendants to go into one of them for treatment. This by no means should ever take the place of seeing your physician or psychologist when you need help; this temple is simply another tool that our Creators have provided for you to facilitate healing while in life, and should be used as a supplement to whatever medical care you're receiving—not as a substitute.

Having said that, visiting this building can be a great help in alleviating or even curing chronic or hard-to-diagnose pain, as well as for preventing health problems. You can also do this for another person such as a sick child or loved one—Francine says that the individual doesn't even need to be aware of it. (This method is now being used as part of my church's prayer line, as we ask that the guide and angels of the afflicted come and get them and take them to the Hall of Healing.) You don't have to know the man or woman you want to help, for just hearing about the problem and genuinely wanting to provide assistance is enough.

You must always remember to take care of yourself first, though. In the same way that a flight attendant will tell you to put on your own oxygen mask before helping another in an emergency, you can't be of much use to others if you're sick yourself. So while you're in the cubicle at the Hall of Healing, ask that all of your organs be healthy; for your hormones to be stabilized; and for all of your other systems, such as the glandular and vascular, to be in perfect working order. If you're aware of a particular problem with your heart, lungs, kidneys, or what have you, concentrate on that, but then ask that your entire body be brought to health and that any pain disappear.

In addition, in this day and age it's a good idea to ask for depression and stress to be lifted and for your energy to rise. Out of 15 or 20 readings I do a day, more than half of those I see tend to be more depressed and tired than they've ever been. I'm sure it's a sign of the times: The wars, gas shortages, unemployment, terrorist threats, and other negative occurrences on our planet prey on our minds, even if it's only on a subconscious level.

Now someone once asked Francine if there was any particular entity whom we should ask for help in the Hall of Healing, and she replied, "Thanks to the Mother God's presence there, you don't need anyone else. There are helpers or attendants to get you settled in the cubicles, and they'll go in with you and take care of you. They are extremely informed and knowledgeable, and the very fact that you're seeking healing gives them permission to access your chart to aid you in any way possible."

While you're in the pyramid cubicle, you can help augment its effects by visualizing the ailment being cured. You always want to put as much emotion as possible into this process, for that's what will activate your own body's built-in self-healing attributes.

Your guide or the attendants can also call in extra help by asking the Archangels, who are the healers of the angelic world, to bring in their green crystal rods to place on any area of your body that needs it. These rods can disperse or suck out illness, as well as help cleanse your body of any residual disease. You can also call on doctors on the Other Side who know about new medical techniques that have yet to appear on the Earth plane. And last, but certainly not least, Azna is there to give solace and healing if your chart allows it—and sometimes even if it doesn't.

You must remember that you've written your own chart, and you may have decided to include suffering with illness and disease—not only to experience it for your own soul's perfection and advancement, but also to allow others around you to grow and learn as caretakers or loving family members. Sometimes the harder test is to have someone you love deeply suffer in life and then not have any significant way to lessen that pain. This takes tremendous tolerance and patience, as well as a spiritually strong soul because the person you care for more than anything is in agony, and there's really nothing you can do about it. I'm sure that if one of your loved ones is suffering, you'd much rather take on his or her burden yourself.

In cases where people write their charts to include illness or disease as primary parts of their life, their plight can be alleviated, but they usually won't be completely cured unless they've written that in, too. Since many don't have this codicil in their charts, this is where the Mother God comes into play.

As stated earlier, Azna is the miracle worker Who *can* change or modify charts to allow recovery, and many times She will do the curing Herself. So stand before Her statue in the Hall of Healing and ask Mother God to embrace you and restore your well-being. The statue will quickly change into a lifelike figure Who will come down off the pedestal and do as you ask.

When She holds you, you might not feel anything right away or just sense a slight tingling sensation, but each time you ask Her to embrace you, it will get stronger and stronger. Not only will your pain subside, but you'll feel a sense of euphoria and then eventually an absence of discomfort altogether . . . and the experience itself will be awe-inspiring. Anytime you have the opportunity to commune with one of your Creators while you're still in this life, believe me, you will never forget it.

(If you'd like to reach this temple through meditation, please turn to page 249 after reading the instructions on pages 181–184.)

Chapter 23

THE TEMPLE OF AZNA
(THE MOTHER GOD)

Now we come to what is probably the most ornate of all the halls on the Other Side. The Temple of Azna has golden columns with gold-leaf lotus patterns at the top (which I've seen replicated in the columns of temples in Egypt), and silvery light glows from its impressive dome.

Inside there are chiffonlike veils of every color, and a light breeze seems to blow them back and forth constantly. There are also wondrous stained-glass windows that go from the floor to the ceiling (which is probably close to 100 feet high), depicting all of the continents, including Atlantis and Lemuria, along with almost every type of animal and human in creation. As you watch, these windows change, and appear to move, almost like they're their own Akashic Records in a sort of holographic glass.

The floor is made of a silvery kind of marble that gives off a continual luminescent glow, and there's a beautiful golden cauldron that's at least 50 feet across, taking up more than one-third of the floor's space. This cauldron is so important because it's where all the petitions to our Mother that have been sent by those of us in life end up. Much like Jewish people place their prayers in the so-called Wailing Wall in Jerusalem, most Gnostics tend to write out their needs and wants in letter form to Azna and either put them in a special repository or burn them, which is what I prefer to do because Francine says that fire is energy and lends more power to the entreaty.

So every single prayer and petition to Mother God, even if it's been spoken rather than written, ends up in this gigantic cauldron from which She absorbs them all. Because She is the Co-Creator, of course She knows what we want and need before we do, but unlike the Father God, She is the Activator. In other words, while our Father is constantly emanating love, He is also very static, solid, and unchanging—He is the reason we're held in place, for He is the "Unmoved Mover" or "Prima Mobile." (He also has His own temple, which you can read all about in the next chapter.) Our Mother, however, can create miracles without putting our charts in jeopardy, so it's very helpful to write or verbalize our petitions to Her.

Like the Hall of Healing, the Temple of Azna features a statue of Her inside. The one here is probably the largest on the Other Side, measuring at least 60 feet high. Yet while most of the other statues show Her in Her armor, this one depicts Her in a beautiful, flowing, and filmy floor-length dress, with Her ever-present sword in Her right hand.

This statue at first appears to be constructed of the same material as the one in the Hall of Healing, but then it periodically changes colors from ebony to gold, purple, green, and then to white. And if a soul asks to see and talk to Her, the stone will immediately begin to change colors, and the eyes will look right at him or her. It is at this point that She will come down off of Her pedestal and come to life, in all Her love and glory!

The Mother God can of course appear in any form at any time or place She chooses, but the writing or verbalizing of petitions and prayers and the visiting of Her temple and the Hall of Healing are the two main ways of making contact with Her that I know of. She considers our Home and the Earth plane to be more in Her domain of responsibility; and when a psychic channels information, it may come from the Father God or his or her guide, but it mostly comes from Azna.

Francine Shares Some of Azna's Wisdom

When we get to the Other Side, Francine says that we all go to visit with the Mother God often, and her human shape is just like ours when She interacts with us. Of course She can take on a different appearence if She chooses and has been seen on holy days by the billions over there in the form of a giant smiling face in the sky, giving out Her love and affection. Francine explains that when She talks to us, the feeling of love and concern is just indescribable, and Her power is so palpable that the atmosphere seems to crackle with it.

My guide says that Azna gives speeches about once a week in our time on all subjects, especially theology. She is referred to as the "Great Infuser" and chooses to keep a human form when dealing with Her creations, while the Father God will only take human form for brief periods or special occasions because His energy and power sustain all of Creation. These are just different approaches that They take, as She prefers to interact with Their creations in a more hands-on manner, while He chooses not to intervene. And since They are God, They both can be in an infinite number of locations at the same time.

Francine said that she recently attended a lecture our Mother gave on how creation started, and countless entities attended. My guide explained that while she'd heard a lot of these facts before, naturally there are always new questions arising from the Other Side's researchers, which then brings up more information. God knows I understand how this goes: As soon as I think that my ministers and I have exhausted a subject, someone in a research trance or at a salon will ask something that sets us off and running again to find new or updated information.

I asked Francine to give me a synopsis of what she heard from Azna, and what follows is her report:

> The story on your side of Genesis, that God made the world in seven days, is a metaphor. Our Father and Mother did make Earth, as They made all the galaxies in the universe you currently reside in. (Remember that humankind has only seen a very small

portion of this universe with its thousands of galaxies and trillions of stars and planets—it is so vast that it is basically incomprehensible to your finite minds.) However, They have also made 43 other universes, which are separate from each other and are like giant bubbles or circles so that they have no end.

We can't visit these other universes because our own cosmos is so vast that we could spend eternity just exploring it alone, so there's no need for us to visit any other. When asked if these universes overlap or are parallel to this one, Azna said no, each one was individual unto itself. They are much like ours, except most are larger; they even have their own Other Sides, which are comparable to our own. And we are welcome to visit any part of our own cosmos—we can travel to any planet in Andromeda, the Crab Nebula, and others so far out that while She and our Father have names for them, even we on my side are not aware of them yet.

Azna said that nothing is illogical in creation, and that it mirrors life and death: Suns come into being and go out in a supernova; planets support life, and then get to the point where that life ceases to exist or adapt; and everything is constantly changing, evolving, and regressing. Only the reality of the Other Side is ever constant and stable. The Mother God went on to say that the words *created* and *time* are misnomers, explaining, "Everything in creation has always existed, for creation has no beginning and no end. There is no such thing as time because everything has, is, and will happen all at once. As God I am the past, present, and future; and each of you is a part of Me and therefore past, present, and future as well. Each of you is like a molecule of My body . . . I experience what you have experienced, what you are experiencing now, and what you will experience; and all that experience is already residing within Me. So everything that is always was."

Azna said that not only do we each have our own individual charts, but the universe and each inhabited world has a chart, too. Like us, Earth has gone through many evolutions to support life. All planets that support life were either covered with ice or molten lava until their orbits came into the right position for life to thrive, as Earth has endured ice ages, volcanic eras, and others in which certain species such as dinosaurs have come and gone, and the planet's orbit around the sun has changed.

When asked if the reincarnation schematic will ever end, our Mother answered, "Not completely," for there will always be souls with their free-will choice who want to experience life on another world in another galaxy. She did say that Earth was coming to the end of *its* schematic, however, and that no other planet will be quite like it again. So those entities who prefer not to incarnate but rather stay on the Other Side and learn, do research, orientate, and the like will have a harder time perfecting or expanding their souls unless they go to a place that has negativity they can overcome, thus becoming more elevated from the experience. She continued to say that those who don't face the negativities of life *can* advance their souls, but it is an inordinately long journey on a road fraught with hard study, in comparison to those who incarnate. She says that's why most entities choose to come down and suffer or survive—they really want to get into the thick of emotion to learn faster.

Azna holds these theological meetings regularly, and just being in Her presence is like nothing I can ever describe. While we always have a feeling of bliss and euphoria over here, to be in the presence of our Mother makes our souls swell even more.

* * *

Francine says that the Mother God is very active with the Council, and She attends many meetings in which spirit guides make petitions for their charges. Her army is the phylum of angels called "the Thrones," and She can just point or think them to a place to give someone extra protection and help. These angels aren't necessarily militant, but they do carry swords (which look like Hers but not as ornate) that they use to fight darkness or evil and fend off psychic attacks. It's funny that the Archangels such as Michael are often depicted with swords when they actually carry healing wands. The Thrones are our Mother's fighters of evil, bringing us protection from the Other Side when we need it.

For example, a woman once spoke up in our church to say that she'd been walking to her car after working late when all of a sudden a man with a knife jumped out at her. She screamed, "Azna, help me! Thrones, come!" not caring what she sounded like. A golden cloud immediately formed that was so thick she could hardly see the man, who seemed to be looking above him before he turned and ran. Only after she was safely in her car with the doors locked did she see the outline of maybe ten glowing angels and a beautiful woman, all of whom were holding swords. Wouldn't you love to find this guy and ask him what *he* saw?

I also heard from a man who told me that he'd reached the Temple of Azna in meditation and asked for Her help. He swears that She counseled him on his miserable job, even giving him specific instructions on how to take a loan out on his house and start a body-shop business. He did so, and is now more successful and happy than he's ever been.

In the Temple of Azna, you can ask for advice, protection, healing, and many other things. This doesn't negate the Hall of Healing or any of the other temples, but what greater blessing could you have than being in the presence of our blessed Mother? I feel that religion has failed by placing our Divine Parents so far away from us that we feel unworthy to see or speak to Them. No wonder we feel like orphans who are abandoned in a place of hell. Visiting this temple and feeling Azna's loving embrace will take such negativity away for good. (If you'd like to do so through meditation, please turn to page 251 after reading the instructions on pages 181–184.)

۞ ۞ ۞

Chapter 24

THE TEMPLE OF
THE FATHER GOD

I feel that this is by far the most interesting temple because of how it has impacted the architecture of this world. As I've said many times before, everything on Earth has first been created on the Other Side, whether it's research, teachings, beliefs, inventions, medicine, or architecture. That's why the ancient Greeks, Romans, and Egyptians copied what they remembered from our Home.

One of the prime examples of this carryover is the Temple of the Father God, for it is a gigantic golden cathedral. When Francine told me about this, I immediately thought, *No wonder we have these enormous edifices on our planet that glorify God.* I personally think it's ridiculous to have them here on Earth when the original stands on the Other Side—especially when you realize that all the money used to build these huge churches could be better used to take care of the poor. After all, Jesus never had a cathedral.

Then I asked Francine if, when Jesus said, "In my Father's house are many mansions," he was referring to all the temples we weren't aware of on the Other Side. I'd previously felt that he was speaking of different lifetimes. She said that both meanings were actually right.

Now while the Temple of the Father God is totally gold, with golden doors and even pink-gold spires that rise hundreds of feet in the air, it doesn't have a cross on top. And instead of saints or "holy pictures" on its stained-glass windows, there are scenes depicting life's hurdles or human endeavors: a mother holding a child; people gathering around a departed loved one; words of wisdom by the holy messengers or messiahs, including "the Golden Rule"; a person giving bread to the hungry; someone saving a child . . . and on and on it goes.

You don't grovel, bow your head, or kneel when you go into this golden sanctuary; on the contrary, you enter proudly, with your head held high. The inside of this temple isn't ornate, except for the golden pillars and a type of altar that seems to be surrounded by a golden mist. There are three steps leading up to the altar, which is made of golden marble and has huge gilded candlesticks on top of it, in which the candles are always lit.

There is a faint smell of incense and a soft breeze that seems to blow through this space, and it's unusually quiet. No matter how many other entities are in there with you, you feel that you're alone with your God. Whether you know Him as God, El, Jehovah, Yahweh, or Allah, it really doesn't matter, for He is the all-loving and all-sustaining Father.

While you're in this hall, the feeling of being loved almost overpowers you; and you quickly find yourself in an altered state of rapture. Of course you feel love and bliss elsewhere on the Other Side, but as Francine says, it's more intense than you could ever imagine in the Temple of the Father God. The power, goodness, and awesome love felt here is so overwhelming that most people can't stay too long because the ecstasy and euphoria are just too much to handle. If you visit the hall in meditation, you'll be able to capture these sensations to a degree—you'll receive strong feelings of love and joy and even the loss of depression—and it's as close to being there as is possible on Earth.

When you approach the altar, Francine says that the Father can show Himself, but He chooses not to hold the visage long because it's so powerful. He appears as a beautiful young male, but the light around Him is so bright that it hurts your eyes. Although He won't be visible for long, you still can talk to Him. He is mostly philosophical in scope and just speaks of love—He can counsel you, but Azna is the one Who gives advice of a more personal nature.

Behind the altar is a huge curtainlike substance that's iridescent in all manner of colors but is predominantly gold. A golden mist surrounds and encompasses it, and you can see the curtain between breaks in this hovering mist. This is the entrance to the seventh level, where created entities of God can choose to go back into "the Godhead," or uncreated mass. For the finite mind's understanding, this is the part of the Divine from which the entirety of creation emanated in God's now. It's also where all dark entities will go when they're absorbed back into Him to be neutralized and purified after the reincarnation schematic is finished.

Francine told me that anyone can view the seventh level, but most don't care to or don't feel comfortable with it. She only went once herself out of curiosity, and the experience was very disconcerting. She said that behind the curtain there is a cloudlike mass of ever-changing colors in which it seems as if millions of floating faces appear and disappear all at once, with each countenance only briefly manifesting before fading away. While my guide wasn't frightened, and she still felt the overpowering love of God during the experience, she didn't look for long.

In more than five decades of conducting readings and meeting thousands of people, I've only known one person who actually wanted to go to the Godhead to lose his identity, and that was a priest who was the head of a university's theology department. As you might imagine, most people want to keep their bodies and individual identities. Francine says that from what she knows about the seventh level, it is a euphoric state, but no friend of hers has ever elected to stay there. She says she knows of a few souls who have, and they seemed to be loner types.

However, anyone can choose to enter the seventh level, even if he or she has a soul mate. You see, the soul mate won't mind because that soul will want the person to achieve the chosen level of happiness and perfection. People often have the wrong idea about soul mates—they have individual lives, and just because they were made together like twins, that doesn't mean they can't follow their own path . . . especially if they choose to attain perfection in different ways.

Visiting the Temple of the Father God is a wonderful and marvelous experience. To be in the Divine presence of our Father, with His constancy and love, is everything we could ever ask for. After all, because of Him, we are all in existence forever. (If you'd like to reach His hall through meditation, please turn to page 253 after reading the instructions on pages 181–184.)

Meditations for Visiting the Temples

INTRODUCTION TO PART IV

As I've already mentioned, we can visit the wonderful edifices mentioned in these pages anytime we wish, and one of the most effective ways to do so is through meditation. (The only exception is the Temple of Levels, which is a meeting place for residents of the Other Side.) We always want to go over with a purpose, so it's best to program ourselves with specific questions to help us resolve any problem we might have before we begin the exercise.

What follows are some helpful hints to ensure that you get the most out of the experience—so do take the time to review them before you do any of the meditations in this section.

Becoming Relaxed

Before you begin, it's important that you are completely comfortable. To that end, try to wear loose and comfortable clothing, and do your meditations in an environment that is neither too hot nor too cold and is as quiet and private as possible. You can either sit with your hands on your thighs in an upward position (to receive positive energy) or lie down in a "prone" position on a couch or bed.

One of the keys to meditation is relaxation. When you meditate, you'll go into what is commonly called the "alpha state," which means that your normal brain waves will slow down, thus allowing your subconscious mind to come more into the foreground. You may wish to record a relaxation process on a tape recorder that helps you get into an altered state of consciousness to prepare for your meditation. An example of such a process is below (but feel free to modify it, use your own words, or employ any other technique that helps you relax):

Get in a comfortable position, and take three deep breaths and exhale them slowly. Focus on your toes and feet and tell them to relax. Then go to your ankles and tell them to relax. Now go to your calves and tell every muscle and every ligament and every tendon to relax. Feel your knees and your thighs losing all tension and stress. Then go to your pelvic area and relax all the muscles, tendons, and ligaments. Notice how you can feel every fiber in your stomach and chest area relaxing.

Next go to your shoulders, upper arms, elbows, forearms, wrists, hands, and fingers . . . feel the muscles throughout these areas becoming free of all stress and tension. Now go to your neck area and face and finally to the top of your head—tell all the muscles to loosen up.

Everything is now so relaxed that you feel perfectly comfortable. Surround yourself with the white light of the Holy Spirt and ask that your spirit guide and angels gather around and attend to you. You are now ready to begin your meditation.

Using this Book's Meditations

When you're meditating to get to the temples on the Other Side, there are a few things to keep in mind. For example, try not to load yourself up with a multitude of concerns at once—if you successfully confine yourself to one issue per visit, you'll find that your answers are clearer, more specific, and of greater assistance. And if you give your questions some real thought before you go, you'll be sure to be amazed by the information you receive in return.

I want to be your guide to these exceptional places where you can get so many ideas. Yet while I've thoroughly described the temples and halls in this book so that you can visualize them and have no trouble finding them, I don't want you to feel limited by my words. This is *your* time, so if you see a structure that's a little different from what I described but you know in your heart that it's the same one, please don't worry. What your heart understands to be true is indeed right for you. And keep in mind that as you do the meditations, I will be right there with you . . . you're always safe. (Again, you may find it helpful to speak the meditations into a tape recorder; that way, you can just press PLAY when you're ready and let the words take you wherever you want to go.)

Before each meditation, I want you to thoroughly read it over, then take the time to become totally relaxed. Make sure that you've turned off the telephone and are comfortable all around. Surround yourself with the white light of the Holy Spirit, the Christ consciousness, or Mother and Father God, and request that your spirit guide and angels be in attendance.

While we're on the subject, it just stuns me when I hear people say they "can't see anything" when they meditate. Well, it's doubtful that you'll witness everything in this process in the front of your head like a television screen in 3-D living color, but will instead construct your imagery from memory. After all, if you couldn't visualize, you couldn't recognize your mother or even find your way home. If I were to ask you about an old love, could you not describe him or her? Of course you could, because a "memory picture" of what this person looks like resonates in your mind.

It's like the white light of the Holy Spirit: You know what a light looks like and you know what white looks like, so you simply put them together and place it around you. If you've seen the movie *The Wizard of Oz,* you probably remember the ball of light that Glinda, the good witch, floated inside of when she first met Dorothy. The white light of the Holy Spirit would look similar to that.

So after you've performed the relaxation technique on page 182, ask that your guide and angels help you to travel or gain contact with the temple of your choice. For example, "Help me to make contact with the Hall of Healing [or whichever temple you're interested in visiting]." At this point, you'll most likely feel yourself going down the tunnel. You'll begin to see all of your passed-over loved ones and feel yourself hugging them. Please be aware of their faces or the feelings they elicit because they could be individuals from your past lives. Take mental notes, because when I've done these meditations in my lectures or salons, many people have come back and told me that they met their great-grandmother or someone they never even knew in life. Breathe deeply, and just let any visages or feelings come. . . .

As you go through each of the halls individually, you'll begin to see which ones you benefit from the most; and as you move through the various meditations, you'll find that you get a different feeling for each one. Every temple has a specific purpose—while some do overlap, each one can help those of us on Earth get rid of illness or pain or resolve something in particular. I promise you that when you get through each meditation, your spirit and spirituality will rise.

One final note: The more you do meditation, the better you get at it. So if for some reason you don't make contact immediately, don't worry. Just try again—and again, if necessary—and you will break through and have a marvelous experience. Be patient and remember that the benefits of meditation will result in your feeling less stressed; more relaxed; and ultimately *better* overall, both physically and mentally.

Enjoy your journey!

🦢 🦢 🦢

Chapter 25

MEDITATION FOR THE TEMPLE OF ORIENTATION

The beautiful Romanesque Temple of Orientation glows with an iridescent, soft, and lovely white light. As you approach it, you notice two sets of large double doors, above which one set has the word <u>Incoming</u> and the other has the word <u>Outgoing</u>. You enter the incoming doors, which lead to the main portion of the temple. It is very large and divided into two distinct areas, one for incoming souls and one for outgoing.

Again going to the Incoming area, you see an orientator coming forward to meet you and your guide. You are led to a cubicle, where your counselor talks to you very quietly, almost orientating you to what you should do in the next moment. Perhaps what you need to do right now is take a deep breath and realize that everything you have gone through is behind you. Maybe it was a "bad trip," but forget it now. You learned, you are back Home, you are safe, you are with your loved ones, and yes, you had a hard time, but it is all in the past. You can also be sure that you know what a good job you did on Earth.

Your counselor holds your hands and lets you sit quietly for a time. He or she also asks that you just look at yourself and notice how young you are—you are 30 now, and all your earthly pains and disruptions are gone, as are the confusions and heaviness of being in the body.

185

This sensation of euphoria just keeps building within you. This is your homecoming, the feeling of "Oh my God, I'm done. I can't believe I'm through with that test." It is like when you know you are going to graduate from school. All of a sudden everything negative washes away from you . . . all of the anguish you have suffered becomes a vague memory.

It is almost impossible to bring physical and mental pain over to the Other Side with you. You know it was there, you know you learned from it, but it no longer exists. Just being in this place, with your guide perhaps standing with his or her hands on your shoulders, and hearing your guide and counselor tell you what a great job you did, how happy they are, and how grateful they are that you went through this because there are so many people who observed your life and learned from it . . . it is so wonderful.

You have this feeling of serenity, this feeling of total joy and completion. That is the operative word, <u>completion</u>—you have completed your journey, you have learned for God, and you are finally back Home.

It is so marvelous to know in this life that we still can visit our true Home, so remember that you can come back here as often as you wish.

Now take a deep breath and come back all the way back to yourself. Feel rejuvenated as you come out on the count of three: one . . . two . . . three.

Chapter 26

MEDITATION FOR THE HALL OF WISDOM

The Hall of Wisdom is like a cathedral, with towering columns and a beautiful stained-glass skylight that is absolutely massive in scope. You notice a multitude of white cushioned benches inside that are scattered about the enormous floor of exquisite marble. You are aware now that you have on a very filmy garment, which can be white or any color you choose.

You move over to a bench and sit down. All of a sudden you notice that there is a large convex glass that appears out of the floor. This is the "scanning machine." You view every event, action, episode, and emotion of your just-lived life in vivid color and in stereo. You sit there very quietly with your hands folded, yet you can stop and start the scanning machine at any time. You are not in a subjective mood now, but rather are objectively going over the things that made up your life on Earth. Review anything that is bothering you now.

Realize that you are in the presence of the Divine and that no one is judging you except yourself. It may seem painful at first to go over a divorce or a death, for example, but you begin to see now how all of the pieces fit together like a gigantic puzzle. For example, if you had a terrible illness, bring up the fear you experienced and how you came out of it. You can even view your own death, and by doing so, you can understand how insignificant it really is.

Most of the time people only want to see up to this present time in their life, which is just fine, but really try to see how you can work through your issues. If you have an estranged family member or friend, for instance, you can see why it was never meant to be. All of a sudden lightbulbs go off everywhere. Instinctive knowledge of why something did not work becomes clear: Was he hateful? Was she really mean? Was he a user? Was that child unappreciative?

I advise that if this is an especially painful situation, you keep going over and over it because doing so helps to flatten the emotion. It removes the shards of glass that seem to pierce your heart. It dulls the hurt, much like watching a horror movie repeatedly. You have seen it before, you know what is coming, and it is no longer scary.

As you are scanning, stopping, rolling back, and going over things in your life without judgment, you sense your guide placing his or her hands on your shoulders. Toward the end of your scanning, you feel your angels surrounding you as well. You begin to forgive yourself for anything that you need to, seeing how everything fits into the learning pattern. You might even think that some things are silly, ridiculous, or just plain laughable now. While you might not have originally seen the humor at the time, you do in this moment.

You sit there very quietly, taking in the serenity of the golden light that surrounds you and the angels and guides who love you. You bask in an uplifting of spirit, of pride and accomplishment, coming away with the feeling that you were not nearly as stupid, bad, rejected, abandoned, or maligned as you thought you had been. You are so proud of the things that you went through because you learned. You watch how your demeanor changes into one of strength after reviewing a horrific episode. And what is even more amazing about the scanning machine is that you can actually see the colors in your aura change from maybe a muddy hue to a bright one or from angry to peaceful.

Your guide is talking to you about different events that you would like to discuss, rationalizing why it was written or why you did what you did, or reminding you that you were not off track. You walk out of this beautiful temple, down the steps, and into a joyous reunion with your loved ones.

Remember that you can go to this scanning machine as many times as you want. It is not because you need to do so to stay on track, because you would not have even have picked up this book if you were off track. More often you will discover that there was no other way you could have dealt with a particular experience because it was all preordained by you. Sure, there may have been some events you could have handled with more panache, but you went through it, and that is what you pat yourself on the back for.

When you are ready, come back, all the way back to yourself, feeling absolutely marvelous, better than you have ever felt before: one . . . two . . . three.

Chapter 27

MEDITATION FOR THE HALL OF JUSTICE

The Hall of Justice is a sanctuary where the revered Council of Elders meets to advise all of those in need. It is designed in a very beautiful Romanesque style of architecture, with large entrance pillars and a great golden dome. As you approach this temple, you are very aware of the statue of Azna, which is glorious in its beauty and awesome in its scope. It is perhaps 50 feet high and shows our Mother God in all Her regal glory and in full battle regalia, which is a metaphorical expression of Her constant fight against negativity and evil. She has shining armor covering Her bosom and upper torso, and armored leggings up to Her knees. She carries a magnificent sword in Her left hand that is pointed toward the ground, while Her right arm is lifted up as if urging Her army of Thrones onward.

Next you note the famous grounds of the Hall of Justice, which feature what are arguably the finest cultivated gardens on the Other Side. As far as your eyes can see, there are paths, benches, alcoves, niches, ponds with koi, waterfalls, footbridges, creeks, and fountains; as well as a dazzling array of flowers, bushes, and trees of every conceivable type or species that you could imagine . . . and some that you could not. And the colors are just outstanding everywhere.

When you enter the Hall of Justice, you feel a sense of serenity. Unlike all of us who are 30 years of age on the Other Side, the Elders of the Council tend to have white or gray hair (and in the case of males, beards). You note that all of the Council members wear a gold medallion around their necks to designate their stature and to help you distinguish the few of them who choose not to take on an older visage.

As you stand there, you are very aware that the function of the Council is basically to advise you. While you have been helped by your guide, you know that the Elders never judge but are always there for those who seek help or counseling. There is no negativity of any kind in that room.

The Elders sit in a square, and you walk in so that you can see people all around you. You are there to ask them any question—maybe it is something that you do not know anything about in this life, or something you have not experienced and yet are afraid of. You might ask them why, for instance, it was so difficult to go through the death of a child, even though you chose it. Since they are very apt to address anything that is on your mind, do ask them whatever you are concerned about. You may find that one of them stands up and is a spokesperson for the others and gives you a valid reason for what you went through, while also reminding you of what your chart read and that sometimes we all wish we had not written some things in there in the first place.

You are surrounded by love and the spirit of consent, as well as an incredible sensation of being lifted up and appreciated—a feeling of loyalty, commitment, and even gratitude on the part of the Council. You see that by going through what you did, so many others were able to learn from your experience. And as you stand there, you are able to verbalize your worries, concerns, feelings of rejection, abandonment issues, and control (or out-of-control) issues, almost like you would with a therapist. The Elders explain that you chose those things, but then they counsel how you can get a better grasp of it, how to deal with it, and how to work it. It is similar to clay: You can keep kneading and kneading or rolling and rolling it, and nothing will come of it. Yet they show you that if you can start carving from that clay, you can make things happen. Even though you have a preordained chart, you can elongate, flatten, and delay things. They show you how to expedite what you need to . . . and again, you receive no criticism.

The Council is so powerful that the longer you stand there, the braver you get, and the more you are able to verbalize and get answers (even more than you may get from your guide) to questions such as "Did I do the right thing? Did I elevate? Did I complete?" And you will be told that of course you did. They might say that you could have done certain things more easily, but you are certainly not at fault. This is not an assessment center. There is justice, wisdom, harmony, consoling, and counseling, but never judgment. Nothing negative like judgment exists on the Other Side. So you stand there with your guide and even your loved ones if you wish them to. Most of the time, however, this is all kept between you, your guide and angels, and the Council.

After you receive your answers, you may feel like going out and wandering in the garden or standing before the gorgeous statue of Azna, because you probably just want to be alone now. You have had your joyous reunion with your loved ones, and you can always go back to it. Maybe you want to sit in the garden beside a beautiful koi pond or walk on a path through the roses that are as big as basketballs, as you sit with the realization that is coming from deep in your heart: <u>My God, I'm back Home again. I am in the presence of long-forgotten dreams and my dear loved ones . . . yes, I am truly Home again.</u>

When you are ready, come back, all the way back to yourself, feeling absolutely marvelous, better than you have ever felt before: one . . . two . . . three.

❦ ❦ ❦

Chapter 28

MEDITATION FOR
THE HALL OF RECORDS

The Hall of Records is a gigantic Romanesque building with many large columns surrounding its entire perimeter and a huge, towering dome on its roof. As it is probably the largest structure on the Other Side, it is able to house miles and miles of corridors that contain seemingly endless rows of shelves and storage areas with every kind of book, disk, tape, chip, and scroll imaginable, along with high-tech devices that have yet to be invented on Earth.

Yet as you walk into this beautiful hall, you immediately know where to go. Sometimes it is not always possible to find or read the chart of those closest to you, but I have found that as time goes on and the veil gets thinner, people are able to read more and more. So find out about your loved one if you can, as it is a wonderful experience. You are not being nosy, because if something is considered private, you will not be able to see it.

You can also visit the living-records section, which lets you feel as if you are actually part of a moment in history. For example, if you want to go back to a life in Victorian England— well, you can actually punch a button and get into that world. This is also a fantastic way to find out about your past lives.

While you are in the Hall of Records, you have a feeling that your whole existence is like a gigantic book and that each chapter lends itself to the next one: The good, bad, exciting, and dull all culminate in the end. And remember that all lives going over to the Other Side automatically make for a happy ending.

Be sure that you take away from here the feeling of the continuum and infinity of life, along with the grace that God gave you to survive on this planet, where you are very blessed to have come. Even though you may think it is a hellhole, keep in mind that it is where you chose to come to learn.

When you are ready, come back, all the way back to yourself, feeling absolutely marvelous, better than you have ever felt before: one . . . two . . . three.

Chapter 29

MEDITATION
FOR THE HALL
OF RESOLUTION

The Hall of Resolution is a glorious temple. It is fairly large and Romanesque in style, with huge pillars at its entrance. Its entryway is lined with gold and leads to a big oval-shaped room with beautiful marble floors. In this room is a lovely, ornate table that seats six to eight people, and you walk up toward it. You notice a small group of Elders seated at the table, and you pull up a chair or stand before them. You lay your concerns out for them much like you would to a therapist, except that rather than matching your questions with more questions, they actually give you solutions.

The group has your chart in front of them and can give you all kinds of information without disturbing it. They say something to the effect of "This is the only way you can resolve the problem"—it might be to back off or go away. What is even more important here is that you are given the grace, stamina, and strength to deal with your issue. That is why you go to this temple in the first place.

If you are dealing with a legal matter, for instance, the Elders might advise you to let it go or get another lawyer. They may tell you something that you never thought of or that could have taken you longer to realize, but in the Hall of Resolution you can expedite the answer.

Maybe you just want (as I have) to whine and tell them about your life. They are very sympathetic and also constantly in the state of reminding you why you are doing this, why you went through something, or why you <u>must</u> go through it—like Jesus at Gethsemane, who asked of God that the experience he was about to endure be removed from him.

You can scream, yell, throw a fit, or be irate; yet the Elders are always very quiet, patient, and understanding. It is even better, I think, than a confessional. The sympathy and enlightenment you receive here is far beyond anything you could ever imagine. Take care to listen to their responses, because the Elders will speak to you either telepathically or with words. You can come to them with anything you want, stay as long as you need, and go there as often as you wish.

When you leave this hall, you will come away with a feeling of resolution, knowing that what you have learned will make your life easier. You understand that you now have a place to go where you are understood better than anywhere else, and where you can truly be lifted up and sense your spirituality. You can visit whenever, and however long, you would like.

When you are ready, come back, all the way back to yourself, feeling absolutely marvelous, better than you have ever felt before: one . . . two . . . three.

Chapter 30

MEDITATION FOR THE HALL OF REMEMBRANCE

The Hall of Remembrance is not as large as the other temples, although it does share their Romanesque style of architecture. This marvelous building, which is shaped in the round, is where you will gain an insight into things long forgotten.

This is a place where you can get to the very root of an addiction or a problem and pull it out. If, for instance, you have a dependency on drugs, nicotine, or alcohol, you can visit this temple and say, "Please let me go back to the very point where this began." In glowing 3-D color, it will immediately come to you: how it started, how you tried to help, and what good it did, if any. "Oh," you say, "now I remember—I was trying to rescue him," or "I was hoping to escape myself by taking too many pills." You are now uprooting all the negativity.

Maybe there is a memory of something that has been eating away at you. This is where you can go back to find the cause of abandonment, feelings of rejection, wanting to control, low self-esteem, or even physical problems or inadequacies. In remembering, the lightbulb goes off; once you remember, you can release the issue. You can visit the point of entry and pull it out by the roots as if it never existed, as if it had never been there.

So ask any number of questions about phobias, addictions, why you left so-and-so, why you did what you did, why you got addicted, and why you were afraid. It will become crystal clear in your mind so that you can rinse it out of you. You are not erasing the memory; you are getting rid of what created it in the first place because you do not need it anymore. You went through it, you experienced it, and now you are done with it.

Stay in the Hall of Remembrance for as long as you want and visit whenever you wish. As with the other halls and temples, you can go out into the beautiful gardens and condense and assimilate what you have garnered; or you can turn around and see the beautiful, rosy-colored light illuminating the majestic Romanesque buildings and just feel that you are Home. Even more important, you will know and feel that God loves you.

Now come back, all the way back to yourself, feeling absolutely marvelous, better than you have ever felt before: one . . . two . . . three.

❂ ❂ ❂

Chapter 31

MEDITATION
FOR THE TEMPLE
OF GOD'S MESSENGERS

(**Note:** For the meditation below, you may want to talk to Buddha or Mohammed, but I use Jesus as the example. Please know that this is not intended to negate anyone's belief or insinuate that Christ is somehow superior to the other messengers.)

Even though the Temple of God's Messengers is Romanesque in design, it has a golden dome on top and looks more like a cathedral. Every type of religious symbol is also represented in its beautiful stained-glass windows—the cross, ankh, Star of David, star and crescent moon, bindu, yin and yang, symbol of Allah—you name it. When you visit this hall, everyone is aware of whom you came to see; and as you can guess from its name, its purpose is to give anyone the opportunity to meet and talk to any of the great messengers, messiahs, and holy men and women of creation . . . including some that you might not even know in this life. Being there allows you to be in the presence of the Divine, for all of these messengers are direct reporters from God.

When you go inside, the entity you need comes from behind a golden veil to meet you, and he or she walks with you around this beautiful golden building that is filled with marble accents.

For example, just say that you wanted to see Jesus, who my guide says is very tall and dark complected with big brown eyes and long, flowing dark hair. He would immediately come to you and embrace you . . . and how can I explain what this is like? It is as if you have met an old friend, someone who has always been there for you and gives you courage and enlightenment.

If you are concerned about your spirituality, this is a way to get it back, by going to this temple and touching Jesus—but I am not referring to the hem of his garment because he does not want you to do that. It is very much like the poem in which he says, "If you cannot walk, I will carry you," and instead of four footprints, there will be two. The problem is that some people have elevated him to the position of God, and he never wanted that. That is why the prayer goes: "Our Father, Who art in heaven," not "My Jesus on Earth."

Jesus now makes the sign of the cross on your forehead, throat, chest, and abdomen—these are the chakras he is blessing. After he does this, you both go out the side door to the left and walk in the splendid rose garden that surrounds this temple. The gorgeous landscape features beautiful trellises and arches, along with every type of colored rose imaginable— lavender, yellow, red, pink, white, and on and on. You walk in this magnificent garden with Jesus, or you can stay on one of the marble pews with him. You converse with him and bask in the beauty and serenity of your surroundings.

You might talk over your troubles with him, for simply being in his presence can neutralize negativity. Or you may not even need to speak, but rather just have him hold you in his arms. You can also communicate telepathically if you choose. But please do not ever say, "I am unworthy—I have sinned and do not have the right to approach you." Remember that he knelt to the most beggarly person, and from the poorest to the highest, no one was out of his reach. The only thing he could not abide was hypocrisy . . . but even if you <u>have</u> been hypocritical, you can still come to him.

You feel the electricity from this marvelous messenger who was sent as a direct reporter from God. Talk about feeling as if you are Home! This is your friend, your confidant, your savior—the messenger who has forever brought you love and hope. Remember that he always reminded you: "In my Father's house are many mansions"—and you are truly in that house now.

As you walk along with Jesus, you might be surprised by the insights you get and that all the material things and worries and problems go away because you are Home. You have your hand in that of the messenger who came to save the world with love. You feel such an upliftedness, such serenity, and such a sense of completeness that no one can take away from you. The love that you have for him, and that you feel emanating from him, is the ultimate—you can see why sometimes nuns take vows of marriage, pledging themselves to Jesus. He is certainly the ultimate soul mate!

You leave this temple feeling so renewed and refreshed. Now bring yourself up, all the way up, feeling absolutely marvelous, better than you have ever felt before, on the count of three: one . . . two . . . three.

Chapter 32

MEDITATION FOR THE HALL OF MEDITATION

This medium-sized hall has a long, rectangular shape, along with many columns supporting it both outside and in. It is extremely peaceful inside, with soft blue light that seems to emanate from the interior columns permeating throughout. There is a larger open space in the middle of the temple, but along the sides are small enclosed cubicles where people can go and be alone and tune in to heavenly music or just have silence. Outside there is a waterfall, so you might enjoy having the window open to hear the water running.

This is not a place to go over negativity, your chart, or what you have done. So take a deep breath and feel yourself going through this beautiful building. Feel that blue light—which is soothing, comforting, quieting, peaceful, and harmonious— pulse throughout you. You go into a cubicle and find yourself reclining on a very fluffy chair that is softer than lambs' wool, and you relax. If you choose to leave the window open, you listen to the water running. Put your mind in a place of fragrant meadows, cool streams, and leafy trees. Put your mind on clouds crossing across the sky. Put your mind in a field in which there is nothing but golden daffodils turning toward the sun. Or put yourself near the seashore, feeling your feet in the sand, the sun on your face, and the wind in your hair.

Everything is euphoric; everything is quiet. You have no worries and no cares. Breathing is very important, so inhale, hold it in for a few seconds, and then exhale. Now breathe in for the count of eight: one, two, three, four, five, six, seven, eight. Then hold: one, two, three, four, five, six, seven, eight. Breathe out: one, two, three, four, five, six, seven, eight. Do this about three or four times, for you are bringing oxygen to your brain.

You lie there in this sublime feeling of being in tune, like my grandmother used to say, with the infinite. You are blended now. There are no worries. There are no traumas. You are so far away from violence of any kind, family or legal issues, the everyday hubbub—whatever. It is all so far away from you. No one bothers you here . . . no one can even find you here. You are in communion with God.

As the light breeze from the open window passes across you, you have never been happier. You have this sense of everything being right, of being Home, of being on track, of quiet peace within you. Anxieties, worries, depression, and even past-life traumas fall away.

You might just want to lie there and look out at the waterfall and beyond, where there are mountains with meadows below. It is so quiet and peaceful. You can even smell the air. It is fresh and clean. Maybe you hear a bird chirping. You delight in every single drop that you hear from the waterfall. You feel a pleasant tingling starting at the tips of your toes and coming all the way up your body. Meditation in itself is certainly healing because it quiets the mind in the alpha state, where everything in your body can rejuvenate. So you remind your soul mind that you are the ruler of your body.

Tell yourself that you will be able to take yourself to this place anytime you wish. This is your own private cubicle, where the iridescent light of blue reflects and permeates. You can still hear the waterfall. You can still see the beautiful rose-colored sun shining on everything. And while you are lying there, you feel young, vital, and strong. You even look down at yourself and see just how young you are. Thoughts can flit in and out, but nothing negative stays. It cannot. The blue light is very powerful. It permeates the soul mind and relaxes it. It is almost like you are now in a floating or altered state where everything seems to blend away. It is just you and the universe. Even if you feel as if there is a cloud around you, do not be concerned, because this is a state in which you can astrally go. It is you and the infinite, the infinity of God's love, and you feel that so prevalently in this state of meditation.

You can call on your guides, Mother God, Father God, Jesus, or whoever happens to be your messenger, but you are in a state of almost suspended thought. It takes some practice to actually put up a mental wall to block any negative thoughts that come in, but after a while, you will feel yourself just floating into the Hall of Meditation, where quiet peace exists.

When you are on this planet, it is very important to go to this temple. We have become so jaded. This is like getting your-self back into your own soul's nature of simplicity and taking joy in everything. You can stay here for as long as you want. Then you get up, come out of your cubicle, go through the col-umns, down the steps, and come back, all the way back to your-self, feeling absolutely marvelous, better than you have ever felt before: one . . . two . . . three.

Chapter 33

MEDITATION FOR THE TEMPLE OF RETREAT (THE TOWERS)

What those on the Other Side simply refer to as "the Retreat" is made up of two large twin buildings that are primarily constructed of dark blue glass. The Towers are set a little bit behind the other halls, and each of them is about 60 stories high and has many rooms. The rooms themselves are comfortable but fairly sparse, containing a downy-soft recliner, lots of books, and a chair that is next to a table laden with paper and writing implements. The only adornments are vases full of fresh, lush flowers, which give off a wonderful potpourri of scent that seems to fill each room.

Now, you do not take your guide or your angels in with you, for it is just you in communion with the tranquility. You can ask for a room that faces the ocean, the mountains, the gardens, or a waterfall. Personally, when I go to the Towers, I like to overlook the ocean or a waterfall because I love water so much . . . you may wish to do the same.

Enjoying the serenity, you take in the meadows, the streams, the lakes, and the mountains. You see all the different-colored birds flying about and listen to the beautiful, heavenly music. You look down and see all the animals and even the people who are moving in and out of the beautiful gardens. You sit there breathing deeply.

You may wish to write, read a good book, or just contemplate. Perhaps you would like to simply breathe and relax. Being alone with your thoughts and your God in the Towers is so rejuvenating. There is such a feeling of peace, with no depression in sight. Any self-defeating notions such as "I should have done this," "I didn't do that," or "I wish I would have . . ." vanish, as you just live in the moment.

I think that this is what is so marvelous about the Other Side—living in the moment. There are no feelings of "I wonder what is going to happen to me in the future." All the things that have happened to you are in the dim past. You have now retreated into yourself to heal and to get away from the hubbub. Even though you love all of your friends and family members, it is sometimes so nice to just be alone.

The Temple of Retreat is one of the places where you can get lost in the euphoria. It is almost like you become one with the universe—with the plants, animals, water, mountains, trees, and on and on—and you truly understand the concept of eternity. You know that nothing is wiped away or lost. Everything is where it should be.

You can stay at the Towers for as long as you want. (In fact, some people have remained there so long that their guides have come in and asked if they would like to come out and mingle.) But there is never any pressure for you to leave, and you can do so whenever you want. When you are ready, come back down out of the Towers. Your mind is so clear now, almost as if you have given it a wonderful bath and rinsed away all the dirt that it has collected. Your soul mind has sprung forward and sparkles now, and you see everything so sharply. Going to the Temple of Retreat helps you escape your stressful world and makes you feel as if you have replaced your dirty glasses with crystal-clear lenses.

On the count of three, bring yourself back, all the way back: one . . . two . . . three.

Chapter 34

MEDITATION FOR THE TEMPLE OF LEARNING

The Temple of Learning looks Egyptian in design, with an obelisk on its grounds and exterior colonnades featuring lotus decorations that are ringed in a dark brown. This building also has smaller windows and is more austere looking than the other halls, although it does have embossed wooden doors, which feature writing in hieroglyphics, cuneiform, and various languages. As Francine says, every thought that humankind has put down historically, musically, romantically, scientifically, and more is found here, including every single manuscript, the Rosetta stone, all of the lost books of Alexandria, and every written word.

As you enter this temple, you notice that there is so much rich wood, including mahogany columns along the sides, and it is so polished that you can almost see your reflection in it. You are immediately met by a facilitator in a beautiful white robe. You might be reminded of a librarian, except that this is a very advanced entity. You realize that you have been here before. You might even work in this facility on the Other Side if it feels familiar to you. In fact, in any of these temples or halls, a feeling of familiarity may be an indication that you work in one of them when you are Home.

You can now find out something about other people and how they would affect your life. Ask the facilitator to help you understand what made Attila the Hun or Salome do what they did. Or say you wanted to know about Thomas Jefferson— well, you are able to read, absorb, or be infused with everything about his life. You might be surprised by how much you begin to know about somebody by going to this hall. This is not a place for your own benefit or to learn more about yourself. While you <u>could</u> do so, right now it is more important to find out about the lives of great founders, elders, philosophers, or writers, and what they accomplished.

Now do not just go in and say that you want to know every- thing about all the philosophers all at once. Choose Socrates, for instance, and see if you can see or sense how he felt before he died—that is, what his mission was. The facilitator will either tell you or lead you to a place where you can obtain the facts yourself. What was the Revolutionary War about? Or see if you can learn more about the fighting that happened between Egypt and Rome, or what life was like on Atlantis. Any information you want infused, shall be.

Now begin to see or feel the intricacies of each chart that winds through everyone else's. Someone clear back in antiquity could have had a part in your life—as Francine always says, "We are like golden beads strung around the neck of God." Each life builds on the other. You see, for example, that Mark Twain went bankrupt at a very old age yet pulled himself out. By view- ing and assimilating this knowledge, you are helping <u>yourself</u> learn from his experiences. Yet not everyone has to be famous . . . in fact, there are many helpful nuggets in this Temple of Learning that have never been written down.

I am convinced that visiting this hall will increase your mind's power and keep it from getting stagnant, even if you just go and sit in the presence of the great knowledge that seems to permeate every fiber of this very large building. While the windows are small, they give off a rosy glow to everything. By simply being there, you feel as if your very pores are absorbing knowledge. Just to bask in all the information that we thought was lost yet is here is wonderful. Stacks and stacks of scrolls, books, and all types of pictorial knowledge are available to enhance, expand, and exercise your mind.

It is so good to know that all of the great libraries in the world are saved. You may want to go in and merely browse, or feel as if this is a contemplative place for you to be. Even if you sit on one of the polished wooden benches and just take in that wonderful smell that we recognize from libraries, you certainly will appreciate this place. See what enters your mind . . . do not let it flood in all at once, but rather allow it to come in easily.

Go to the Temple of Learning many times. Each time you do, ask for aid on a different subject. Let us say that you are having trouble at school with calculus—do not be afraid to go and have a math facilitator come up and help you. You might be amazed the next day that all of a sudden it clicks. Or maybe you never knew about astronomy but would now like to. Certainly you can read about these subjects in this life, but see what asking for infusion on them does. Sit there because the facilitator might not even direct you, but will instead give you a lecture on the subject, which you will then assimilate.

Come back now, reminding yourself that you can return to this temple anytime you want. On the count of three, bring yourself back, all the way back, feeling absolutely marvelous, better than you have ever felt before: one . . . two . . . three.

Chapter 35

MEDITATION FOR
THE HALL OF RESEARCH

The Hall of Research looks like the ancient Temple of Artemis. It is made of pink marble with blue streaks running through it, and it seems to emit a soft white light. While it appears somewhat Romanesque, it is definitely Grecian in design in that it has smaller columns. Yet these columns are 60 feet tall and spaced so that there is plenty of room between them. There is also a large porch on the side of this hall, which is very open and airy inside.

Scientists, inventors, theologians, artisans, historians, writers, doctors, and a host of others do their exploration and experimentation in this building. Countless discoveries in every field of endeavor imaginable originate here, and all entities love to come in for a visit. You will find people working on all types of machinery, writing about various subjects, doing experiments in medicine, and performing research . . . you might even be one of them when you are Home, so you would know this temple very well.

It is marvelous to go here and find out what these people are doing. It is so interesting to see all those working here in what appears to be almost like a beehive, buzzing around everything imaginable from inventions to scientific endeavors in astronomy, astrology, and chemistry. And they do not mind sitting and talking with you about the latest discoveries. Let us say you are working on a paper and want to know something about archaeology. Well, find an archaeologist and talk to him or her. You will get answers to anything here, no matter how ridiculous it may sound. And no matter how far-fetched it may seem, listen intently to what everyone has to say.

To be in the presence of such intelligence and activity is so marvelous. Benjamin Franklin and Leonardo da Vinci are still working on their inventions, but do not be intimidated, for you knew these great minds way before this life. And maybe you were once a great mind yourself! Everyone is approachable. The saints—or those we call saints here on Earth, such as rabbis, priests, and other holy men and women—or anyone who has anything to find out or tell you about—are in this hall.

Even if you are not so much of a researcher, you can still enter this temple. If you are a writer who is stuck, you can unblock yourself here. If you ask a doctor about an undiagnosed illness you might have, see if you get some idea what is wrong with you. Or discover how the planets are lined up and what is happening to Earth itself. Go to an ecologist and find out what is happening with our warming trend. You might be surprised by how prophetic even <u>you</u> get, because there is knowledge over there that is way ahead of what is on the Earth plane. As I have said innumerable times, everything on this planet is first done at Home.

See what is going on with the newest inventions, and observe those working hands that are in the process of doing research. Maybe you only want to look; maybe you want to join in. The inventors, historians, or researchers are so eager to show you what they are working on and may even ask for your advice. It is a marvelous place to be. If nothing else, just seeing the infinity of knowledge that you know will never stop is wonderful. I think it would be miserable if when we crossed over we simply sat on a cloud with a harp. No, it is a working place. You would think with all the inventions, the building would be one big mess, but it is beautiful and clean because everything is neatly kept in its own quadrant or section. Historians, inventors, theologians, and doctors are all in their own section; and they pass their knowledge back and forth.

Take yourself through this temple and visit any branch that interests you. Go to the theology, archaeology, or inventions department; or go to the medical section and see what is going on and being done with AIDS, multiple sclerosis (MS), cancer, heart trouble, diabetes, and other illnesses. Do not be afraid to ask questions—you might not actually hear anyone speaking, but you will understand every word.

So take yourself to the Hall of Research and gain some knowledge. If you are stuck on something, go there and voice your concerns. You might be so surprised to discover that you are more right than wrong. Never be afraid to share the knowledge that you come back with, because years from now you could just be proven right. I know that the prophets could get to this temple, and I am sure that it is where they got some of their knowledge.

You may feel like a kid in a candy store when you see all the new inventions and how happy and enthused everyone is. It is unfortunate that we have lost so much zest here on Earth—if nothing else, you will bring back with you the passion for finding information. The sense that, "Oh, there it is . . . now I've got it . . . the puzzle fits!" is so rewarding. And what is so amazing, as my guide says, is that as soon as you get one puzzle piece to fit, then you find another one. Visiting this temple is so uplifting for the soul. It takes away depression. It takes away boredom. It takes away any feelings of uselessness.

When you are ready, bring yourself back, feeling absolutely marvelous and full of knowledge, utterly prepared to answer questions. On the count of three come back, all the way back to yourself: one . . . two . . . three.

❦ ❦ ❦

Chapter 36

MEDITATION FOR
THE HALL OF NATURE

The Hall of Nature is one of my favorite places to visit. In comparison to the other temples, it is not that big, but it can easily accommodate the studies conducted inside. What is unique here is not the building itself, but rather what lies behind it. In back of this hall are huge compounds that contain virtually every type of natural habitat for both plants and animals. You have various types of woods, from sweltering rain forests to large stands of evergreens and all that falls in between, such as mangrove swamps with towering hardwood trees that rival anything you have ever seen. There are also mountains, deserts, plains, and oceans.

Among these compounds one can spot any species of animal, bird, reptile, and fish that has ever been, including the dodo and all types of dinosaurs. And there are domesticated animals, which of course include the pets that you have had, along with cows, chickens, and horses.

No animal is vicious; no animal is cruel. The lion can truly lie down with the lamb. So you have beautiful leopards walking beside small pigs without eating them. All of these creatures lovingly coexist, domesticated and wild, and wander together throughout groves of fruit trees. You will see animals that you might be terribly afraid of in life come up to you, and you will pet and love them. Having a lion follow you and rub up against your leg like a kitten is a marvelous thing to behold, especially if you are an animal lover.

Many horticulturists are there, creating everything from beautiful Chinese and Japanese gardens with cherry blossoms to very ornate fountains. While there is a lot of artisan work in this area, these souls mostly concentrate on plants, studying and caring for them. This just goes to show that everything God has created is reproduced again . . . it is so amazing.

You take pride in the smells and sounds, and you feel so rejuvenated by this life that is in abundance around you . . . the lush foliage and the vibrant colors. And facilitators are there to help you on your travels. So if you decided to go into an Amazonian-like rain forest, then you could do so. Or if you wanted to visit the ocean, you can just go there. Every type of fish is present, and no shark will bite you. You could float forever buoyantly in the sea, never drowning or getting tired. Even if you cannot swim in this life, you can do it here if you so choose. Or if you wanted to walk on water like Jesus did, then you could do so.

It seems that the dichotomy of the Hall of Nature would be too stark, but it is not. The beauty of human beings and that of nature sort of blend together to take away stress. And it is especially nice, too, to see that nothing is spoiled—the dolphins swim free, there are no cigarette butts or beer cans anywhere, and there is no debris. Everything is pristine and beautiful. Yes, you have people studying in this temple, but you also have people caring for and loving it.

When you walk through these forests, it is almost like you are walking through living, breathing things. These trees and bushes and branches and fruits seem to be alive. Of course, <u>they are</u> living, but it is almost like they are sentient as well.

As a retreat, there is nothing better than the Hall of Nature. Think of how you have felt when you have touched animals, how they can take all the negativity out of you. Can you imagine how you would feel being surrounded by all this foliage and these creatures?

Ask that any heaviness that you are carrying drains out of you after you have taken a trip to this temple. After you do, notice that you are now more rejuvenated and better off than you have ever been before. On the count of three, bring yourself back, all the way back, feeling absolutely marvelous: one . . . two . . . three.

❦ ❦ ❦

Chapter 37

MEDITATION FOR THE TEMPLE OF ARTISTIC ENDEAVOR

The Temple of Artistic Endeavor is probably one of the most beautiful halls from a visual standpoint, as it exudes so many colors—green, purple, pink, blue, and gold. This building is Romanesque in design but only has two gigantic columns framing the front entrance, and it is octagon shaped with different wings coming out of the sides.

This hall contains scale models of villages or types of architecture that have long been lost to us in the modern world, along with cave drawings, sculptures from ancient Egypt, and creations we have not even heard of that go back to humankind's very beginning. But what is most exciting is that this hall houses the originals of all of Earth's famous paintings and works of art, such as Michelangelo's <u>David</u> and the Venus de Milo (with her arms intact), and many statues of the ancient gods and goddesses. You can even see what the Colossus of Rhodes or the Hanging Gardens of Babylon looked like. I know that it can be difficult to understand how all of this can fit, but just remember that our earthly laws of physics do not apply on the Other Side. So take a breath, go through the large doors with the big golden rings, and enter this huge and splendid building.

There is so much that is magnificent in this temple, with its marbleized floor, its serenity, and the glory that you see all around you. View through the eons of time these exquisite artifacts, which stand as a representation of the beauty humankind can create. I think this is more of a viewing temple where you can go even if you are not interested in artistic endeavors. Whether or not you bring any talent back with you, it is still marvelous to visit this lovely place. Think of this: You can see all the classic works from the beginning of time to the end, and you do not have to spend a dime.

As you go along, stop and look at a few different areas. After all, the temple contains cave drawings, art and hieroglyphics from ancient Egypt, all types of Mayan artifacts, sculptures, petroglyphs, raised or embossed paintings in every material you can think of . . . anything that you have ever heard of (and even what you have not) is there. Every kind of craft exists there as well, from ceramics and pottery to tile work and mosaics. There are huge tapestries, needlepoint canvases, and examples of various kinds of weaving.

While you are walking through, note the pictures of all of the different types of architecture from the beginning of time. Some are even duplicated in miniature versions or on a smaller scale, so you can see what Pompeii was like or view the structures of the early Incans, Mayans, or Aztecs. This is an experience that you truly would not want to miss.

So stroll through this temple at your leisure. This is one time where I am not going to describe every room. I want <u>you</u> to wander around and validate everything, and do not use the word <u>imagination.</u> I am telling you that if you visit this temple enough, you are going to find that you are drawn to certain wings more than others. For example, the so-called ethnic pieces, such as the Japanese, Mayan, German, and Greco-Roman, seem to be in separate wings. Notice how the light plays on the different paintings by Raphael, Monet, and of all the talented artists who have come down through the centuries—including the ones you do not even know about . . . those who have been lost in the sands of time.

If nothing else, a visit to this temple certainly lifts your spirits. After all, you know how great you feel after you have been to a beautiful museum. A facilitator, your guide, and even a loved one can go with you and hold your hand while you walk through the beautiful rooms. As you do, notice if you experience any familiarity, as if you have been here before. This could mean that the Temple of Artistic Endeavor is where you work when you are Home.

You may even ask the facilitator how to do a mosaic or painting. It is very possible to bring forth abilities that you did not have earlier in life during this meditation. As you walk these halls, you have feelings of being so uplifted, and of the infinity and beauty of time. Everything stands as pristine as it did when it was first created.

Stay here as long as you want, musing about the beauty of this location, and then come back, all the way back to yourself, feeling absolutely marvelous, better than you have ever felt before: one . . . two . . . three.

🏵 🏵 🏵

Chapter 38

MEDITATION FOR
THE TEMPLE OF VOICES

The Temple of Voices is smaller than the other halls on the Other Side, yet it probably has the greatest acoustics of them all. The building is perfectly round, Romanesque in design, and all gold: The columns are gold, the steps are gold, the doors are gold, and the dome is gold. In fact, no other temple over there is totally gold like this one—yet it seems to be glowing with a tremendous iridescent, almost fuchsia-colored, light.

My guide says that the Temple of Voices attracts souls like a magnet because the tones and quality of the music are so magnificent. Here you can hear the Cherubim and the Seraphim, or you can listen to a choir of people from this life who have had beautiful voices. An example would be the Mormon Tabernacle Choir or other lovely, harmonious voices you are familiar with. They could be contemporary in nature or even what has not yet been heard on Earth. Everything is melodious and symphonic even though there are so many different instruments: violins, trumpets, French horns, and the like. You might think that the sounds of all these instruments would create a din of noises, but they do not. They do not all play at once; it is a singular sensation.

My guide says you actually "see" the music; that is, you literally perceive colors and notes when a symphony is playing.

The music streams through every molecule of your being so that you are not just hearing with your ears—your entire body is absorbed by this.

It is especially wonderful to hear the angels singing. Their voices are like bells, and some people who have been there have validated this beautiful music by reporting that they often did not even remember what the lyrics were but instead focused on the melodious sounds. I can tell you of so many individuals who have actually looked up in the air during a time of trial and seen and heard angels singing, which then made their own souls sing.

You can have anything you want or need on the Other Side; all requests are granted. So think about what you would like to hear—or even better, leave it up to them. Enter this temple, sit back in your own cubicle, and see the iridescent fuchsia color swirling around you. Now feel the music enter your soul . . . it is making you vibrant, rejuvenating every molecule of your body.

Stay here until you feel more alive than you have ever felt on this planet. Then come back, all the way back to yourself, feeling absolutely marvelous: one . . . two . . . three.

Chapter 39

MEDITATION FOR THE
TEMPLE OF LECTURES

The Temple of Lectures is a multileveled building sur-rounded by a golden gate and fence and topped by an orange dome. Even though it features columns and other Romanesque touches, it has a lot of Egyptian flavoring, including lotuslike designs at the top of the pillars. There is also a large golden obe-lisk behind the hall, which represents the finger of God pointing upward and the channeling of lecture material from Him.

The temple teaches people how to give a lecture, much like the Temple of Artistic Endeavor instructs individuals in drama, but it is also the home base for what we might refer to as the Other Side's "regular orators." So if you need help with public speaking, experts will assist you. Then when you are ready, you may find yourself wanting to give a lecture to the populace. You see, we are always learning when we are Home, so of course you would want to share whatever information you had with your fellow souls.

You can find great lecturers working and studying in another part of the building, and you can hear them speak at any time. Everyone is open to new information over there. Ask your guide to take you to a lecture that interests you. Or if you have a paper to write or there is something you want to know about a certain subject, such as astronomy, say, "Please help me find out about this." Then you will immediately hear Carl Sagan or another expert in the field and get the answers you seek.

It is amazing because you can go to any number of halls on the Other Side and then get together with other entities to talk about what you have learned. You stand around and have a type of party, going over the lecture or brainstorming. Or you go out into the beautiful redwood-forest area to sit in groups and discuss what you have seen or heard.

You can also go into the temple to watch people working on their speeches. They do not have to write them down like we do on Earth because everything is completely assimilated, although they can take notes if they want to. If there is a particular person you would like to hear, ask your guide to tell you when Abraham Lincoln or whoever is talking, and ask that you remember what he or she said when you come out of your meditative state.

Since this hall features lectures by so many writers, teachers, theologians, scientists, and other experts, you might find that you stumble into one by somebody you did not know or did not find interesting before, and then discover that you learned a great deal. Some people get up and talk about their lives and experiences, such as how they overcame years of pain or suffering or what they did to attain a higher level of happiness and spirituality. You absorb the message right away. It is not just empathy—it actually permeates your soul and you see it. It is a sharing or merging of thoughts; therefore, even if you have never experienced MS or Lou Gehrig's disease or whatever it might be, you absorb a lot of knowledge from the speaker.

If you would rather just sit quietly in the Temple of Lectures, you can do so. Relax on the cushioned marble benches and listen to what is being said around you, for you might come back with tremendous knowledge. Immediately write things down in your notebook, even if it is only a few words that will spark some ideas or knowledge later on. You may be surprised by how your mind opens. I am convinced you will never get Alzheimer's if you visit this beautiful building because your mind is always alert here.

Each time you go into one of these temples, whether you realize it or not, you gain more grace, strength, and spirituality. It does not matter if you only stand on the inside of the portals—the very fact that you have made it there will imbue you with knowledge and power.

On the count of three, bring yourself out now, through the doors, down the steps, and back, all the way back to yourself, feeling absolutely marvelous, better than you have ever felt before: one . . . two . . . three.

❧ ❧ ❧

Chapter 40

MEDITATION FOR THE TEMPLE OF MYSTICAL TRAVELERS AND MISSION-LIFE ENTITIES

The Temple of Mystical Travelers and Mission-Life Entities is a fairly small building, and although it is Romanesque in design, it is fairly nondescript compared to some on the Other Side. I think the reason is because, as Francine has told me, mission-life entities and mystical travelers come and go, so they really do not need a habitat or a hall. They basically check in, find out what their assignment is, and then go on. However, this temple is very beautiful. The columns are silvery rather than gold, as is the temple's door and interior—the walls even seem to give off a silvery light.

Mission-life entities and mystical travelers are souls who came to this planet to make it better in some way. Mystical travelers are like our Creators' troubleshooters, while mission-life entities are more tied in to making something specific happen for Them. Most spiritually evolved individuals are thought of as mission-life entities, but they tend to be on their last lives and have gone through many existences in order to attain such a state of evolvement. They are often the ones who help with the orientation process for incoming and outgoing souls. They may also be researchers, teachers, lecturers, counselors, or even spirit guides.

Now, please do not get the idea that the mystical traveler is higher than the mission-life entity. There is no such thing, as everyone is equal in God's eyes. It is only a matter of occupation. Please, please understand that.

Also, do note that while anyone can be a mystical traveler, you should be very careful taking on this role. After all, once that mantle drops, it means that you may be asked to go to any place in the universe that needs help. And you will go there upon God's direction. Even though your home base may be Earth's Other Side, you can also reside on _any_ Other Side, from Andromeda to the Pleiades . . . anywhere. You will be asked to go wherever there is a problem, for mystical travelers are the problem solvers of the universe. (You can still come back to this planet and visit all of your loved ones.)

A great soul with a magnificent amount of courage is required to take on this responsibility because it means that you and your ego have given total submission to God. Do not be afraid if you get to this temple and do not feel like you can do it. No one says, "Tsk-tsk" or "Aren't you ashamed?" because you will be just as respected if you are a mission-life entity. You may want to talk to the Council about this. Francine says that she has seen people go in 40 or 50 times before they finally decide they want to be a mystical traveler, while others never decide to be one.

Let us say that you go in and you _do_ want the mantle to drop. It then does, and you turn around with this imbued courage, as if you have been knighted and are carrying the sword of Azna through the world of negativity. Always remember that the sword makes a cross and is never to create harm. Its purpose is to cut through darkness, ignorance, and bigotry with respect to ethnic groups, sexual preferences, cultural or religious differences, and all the negativity that surrounds those issues. All are equal in God's eyes, and you fight for that truth.

"I am a mystical traveler, and I am proud of it," you say. "I will do God's bidding." You get your mantle in this beautiful temple, and the Council and others then ask you, "Are you sure—do you know what you are letting yourself in for? Do *you know that you have to submit your will, and that you can be asked to go anywhere where there is fighting, where there is malice, or where there is greed?" You say yes and get your assignment.*

The mantle of the mystical traveler is wondrous, because when it drops, it is permanent. Out of millions of souls who have taken this on, that mantle has only been ripped off once. You really have to create a schism for that to happen, because once it is on, it becomes part of your essence. It seeps into your pores, making you willing from this point on to be a mystical traveler for God.

So when the purple mantle drops, you can almost feel it, and it is marvelous. It is as if you have been knighted to be God's Templar and to fight for goodness anywhere that you are directed to go. When you go back to yourself in this life, things will change, I promise you. Irritations will now roll off of you and will not bother you as they did before. You feel as though you truly are on a mission for God.

You walk out of the temple feeling imbued with Spirit. Even if you decided not to take on the mantle of the mystical traveler, you still have a mission . . . a mission of life. You walk past your heavenly hosts, behind whom smiling angels are standing—with beautiful wings tipped in gold, maroon, green, and blue—all the archangels, the Cherubim, the Seraphim, and on and on. Then you go out of this temple and come back, all the way back to yourself, feeling absolutely marvelous, better than you ever have before: one . . . two . . . three.

Chapter 41

MEDITATION FOR THE TEMPLE OF SPIRIT GUIDES

The Temple of Spirit Guides is fairly plain compared to many of the others. While the building does have gold pillars and doors, the rest is made up of unadorned gray marble. Inside is just a huge hall with a large podium and rows of built-in chairs, much like you would find in a movie theater. Lining the hall are the "compatibility meeting rooms," in which people meet their spirit guides and decide if they are the right fit for the individuals' missions or charts.

You go into this temple and walk down the long rows. You enter one of the rooms and sit there, and your spirit guide appears. You realize that your guide is solid, and whether this entity is male or female is of no matter. Males are usually in sort of a Roman-style toga or a robe. Females, on the other hand, generally wear chiffonlike garments. They do not wear miniskirts and boots, trust me—my guide said she has never seen anyone look like that. Not that there is anything wrong with it, but there is a sort of dress code over there in that people like to feel very comfortable.

Your guide sits in this beautiful iridescent room with you. It is not a cubicle as much as it is a bubble, and the bubble changes colors. There is also a very low type of humming sound that surrounds you, and a slight lilac scent wafts by. When your guide comes in, the bubble closes, and you begin to talk. But do not expect the guide's lips to move; you will get these words telepathically.

Your spirit guide has you alone now, and there are no outside influences, noises, or friction. And you are totally, completely comfortable with each other. It is like meeting a loved one. It does not matter what you call your guide, whether it is Jane, Joan, Bill, or Harry. I know people like to know the name of this being, yet it is truly very insignificant.

Ask your guide about your chart, why you hit a snag, or why a particular event happened. If you are facing a custody battle, a legal suit, an IRS problem, or an illness, inquire what purpose it is serving and how you can get out of it. What is the best way to take care of this issue?

Ask if there was any influence that you shared together from a past life. How much did you study together? Your memory begins to roll backward now, and you can see yourself sitting there being geared up for your chart and your incarnation.

You look into the beautiful eyes of your spirit guide, and all of a sudden your road becomes very clear. Your guide can even take out your chart and show you exactly where you are on your path. It is almost like a map: There you are, there you should be, there you will be, and there you will end up. Knowing that you are on track will give you such a feeling of sanctity and righteousness. And you <u>are</u> on track or you would not have come this far. You will be so amazed at how spiritual you have become and how elevated you are.

Yet do not be concerned if you want to argue with your spirit guide, because he or she will always come back to logic and what you are learning for God. You cannot beat that logic, no matter what you say. You could "if, and, or but" it all the way through, yet the chart shows you chose it and you are learning for God. Your guide's love for you is unconditional, so nothing you can do will ever deter that love. So you sit there for a moment to bask in the presence of this beautiful entity in his or her home base.

You also have a memory that you have sat, or will some-day be sitting, where your guide is, giving help and hope to someone else, since the chances of all of us doing a roundabout and becoming a spirit guide are pretty certain. Maybe you have already been a guide; if you have, the memory of your giving counsel to someone or receiving training to help another soul now returns.

If you have yet to be a spirit guide, this also gives you insight into what the training is about. Your guide will even take you out of this round bubble and put your chart up on a board and show you in glowing detail exactly where you came from. You know what is so great about this? Every memory floats up—the good, the bad, and everything that made you who you are.

So this is a good meditation to do when you are trying to remember something. Go back and have the guide put your chart up, like on an x-ray machine, except this is huge—then it can be laid out in pictorial, as well as in written, form. You stare at it and note where you are. You see your road, which is called the "blue line." And you may find that you wiggled a little bit sometimes but are nevertheless right on the mark.

You hug your guide, and you are so happy because you know that you can meet there anytime. You also know you are not really leaving, for even though you go through that door alone, as soon as you come back to your body, your guide will be right there, standing to the right of you as a silent sentinel, never leaving you. So walk down the long hall arm in arm with your good old steadfast friend, who is always there when every-thing else fails.

You pass through the doors of the temple, knowing that your guide has to go around and come in through the other door to get into life to be with you, but it only takes a millisecond. You are never alone. You feel absolutely marvelous, better than you ever have before, knowing that your guide is always there and that you can always go to the Temple of Spirit Guides, realizing that you will learn to be a guide yourself here, and understanding that you can receive solace and comfort. All of this is elevation for the soul, so you can never do it too much.

On the count of three, come back, all the way back to your-self, feeling absolutely marvelous, better than you have ever felt before: one . . . two . . . three.

Chapter 42

MEDITATION FOR
THE HALL OF CHARTS

The Hall of Charts is made of pink marble with only two (gigantic) columns at its main entrance. It is not an enclosed building, but is instead open on all sides so that people can come and go easily. Inside you will find a large hall with lots of seats, along with a spectacular waterfall just inside the main entrance; the falls flow into a great fountain that changes colors.

The building sits back a little from the other temples and is surrounded by lovely trees of every variation. There are no formal gardens, so the landscape forms a natural-wildlife type of refuge. This is where various animals such as deer, squirrels, gazelles, raccoons, and chipmunks tend to be found, meandering about the grounds. It is very beautiful and calming here, as the Hall of Charts exudes the beauty of nature.

It is very important to visit this site because it gives you an idea of being on track. It is like a study hall—sometimes you are with groups of people you are going to incarnate with; other times you will be individually singled out and meet with your guide, the Council, or other influential people; or you can just be by yourself.

You enter this temple and see a large board with all the intricacies of your life: those whom you are going to meet, what is going to affect your life, and especially what you are going to learn. Everything is charted, from the date of your birth to the tragedies you will go through. After more than 50 years of being a practicing psychic, I am convinced that we just say yes to everything because we are in such a state of bliss on the Other Side. Then after we come down here, we are not so sure or else we want to renege on it, much like we do at school where we take on all these difficult subjects because we are so gung ho. Then after we are there for a while, we don't want to take chemistry or algebra anymore.

The Council will advise you, but there is free will, so you sometimes negate their recommendations. It does not matter, though, because you have to stay on Earth. You cannot break your contract. You can chart an easy incarnation or a hard one, but if you are on your last life, you probably chose a really high mountain to climb. It is so great after you get up there and see the view, for the trek down is so much easier.

So take yourself back to where you made your decisions. You might be very surprised to find that you must stop blaming God, for it was <u>you</u> *who charted losing a child or a spouse or having an illness. You probably will not be able to read your chart beyond what you know it to be right now, but you can certainly see in glowing detail how much you really are on track and how much you have learned, along with how much Jesus, the Council, and the angels care about you. And your guide is conversing with you, counseling you, and telling you that he or she will always be there with you and honestly hopes that you will make contact in life.*

Look at your chart up to this point and see that you really have followed that blue line. Now the line might be a little wavy at times, but that is part of living. It is sort of like driving a car and getting sidetracked for a while, and then all of a sudden you look at your map and say, "Oh, okay, now I am on the right road! I was off my chosen path for a while, but now I'm back on my way." You might be a little delayed, but you <u>are</u> *going to get there. You even chart your exit points, which means that you can say no to life at these times, but you will probably* wait until the final one because you want to learn. It is not a smart thing to take an early exit point, although some people can have all their exit points completed by the age of 20.

Next you meet the people whom you will encounter in life. There is a famous guru who once said that everyone whom you meet you have known, and I believe that. You sit in your chair like you are in a classroom with your loved ones, but you can interact with them. Your chart is the major one, and they are secondary players, so after they hear what you have to say, each one takes a turn speaking. Then one of theirs can be the major chart, with you as the secondary player. Not everyone is a primary player in somebody's chart, but they are <u>always</u> primary in the eyes of God.

Everything is intertwined, and it is so intricate. Even the person you give a hand to at in the grocery store is in your chart—so be aware of how the tiniest thing can bring someone else joy. Resolve from this time on until your final exit point that you will smile more, give more hugs or pats on the back, or let people go in front of you in line. Why not do a little extra work? Push a cart for someone, help somebody across a street . . . the responsibility is up to you. Yes, God is there with you, but it is <u>your</u> responsibility to learn.

You now understand what you need to take on to glorify your own soul. If you are really smart, you will say, "From this point on, I want my intellect and emotion to be cemented together so that I will always have a marriage within myself and not be divided against myself." Because when the emotion takes over too much, it floods the intellect. Say that you will be a pillar of light for God, and that you will walk this track to the very end.

Now, with your chart in hand, know that you truly are on track, and if you are not, you know how to adjust it. Look at the board and listen to what the Council says: What were you here to accomplish? What was your theme? Were you a humanitarian or a rescuer? Did you fight for justice? Maybe you do not have to know your theme specifically, but you will live it out, believe me.

Dark entities never care where they are or if they are on track, so do not ask if you are one of them. As Jesus said, only those who seek will find—and you are on a deep search for answers. When you get down to the basics, you are in a school, learning your tests for God, and then you come Home. It is as simple as that. If you make it more complex with dogma and "I should have done this" or "I didn't do that," then you are going to wobble all over the place. Keep it straight and simple. Let no one tell you what to do; let no one take over your life. Keep your eyes on your road.

After you leave the Hall of Charts, you will feel so much better. You can even bring the scroll with you. You are not going to come back to your sitting or prone position actually holding a gold scroll in your hand, but it is almost as if it imprints on your soul and makes it stronger. You know where you are headed and where you have been. You might not know all the ifs, ands, or buts about your future, but you know what you have been through and you know what you can survive. Even if you live to be 120, you know you can make it, for you know how many mountains you have climbed and how many valleys you have crossed, yet you are still standing. Be proud of yourself because you have learned for God.

Take a deep breath and come back, all the way back to yourself, feeling absolutely marvelous, better than you have ever felt before: one . . . two . . . three.

Chapter 43

MEDITATION FOR THE TEMPLE OF PENANCE

The Temple of Penance is not what it sounds like. We always think of penance as having to make restitution for something, but this hall has nothing to do with that. It is not a duplicate for anything you know at church in which you have to kneel down, say rosaries, or flagellate yourself.

This is a much smaller yet Romanesque building that is set back a little from the larger halls. It is, I repeat, not in existence to punish you or show you what you have done wrong or whether you will live another life or not. Francine says that not everyone needs to go there, but you may find a visit to be very helpful.

You view things from your life on a scanner, yet you are now focusing on the experiences that you feel are unfinished, including things you never got to say or explain to someone. It is basically a place to tie up loose ends that might be on your conscience.

With your chart in hand, you can meet with any person you wish to call on, with the specific purpose of working out any confusion or animosity. The idea is to get rid of any of those little pinpricks of life—for example, if you felt that you were excessively rude or did something wrong.

I once spoke to a woman who was so upset because as a child she took a $20 bill out of her mother's purse—insignificant things such as these sometimes seem to get bigger as we get older. We can go to the Temple of Penance and justify what happened with someone; and more times than not, the person does not remember it, does not care, or did not think anything of it when it occurred. Suffice it to say, we need to do this for ourselves.

This is kind of what you might call "the clean-up temple." You will never sweep anything under the carpet, but you will make sure that you get rid of all those little slings and arrows that you might have put out; or the cruelty, the curtness, or the pain you gave someone. In this hall you make sure that you wind all of this up, because it is in your chart and certainly on your scanner.

It is so good to get rid of a lot of the guilt and the feelings that you did something wrong; 99 percent of the time when you go to the Temple of Penance, you will find out that the individual you are anxious about did not even have any feeling about it at all. You may say, "What if the person is still living?" It does not make any difference. The hologram or the spirit of the individual can still be there because even though it is hard to understand, everything is in God's now. While you are there, you might think of more things you would like to clear up than you originally did. You could even write a list so that you are prepared the next time you go to this hall.

When you are ready, come back, all the way back to yourself, feeling cleansed of any past transgressions and so refreshed: one . . . two . . . three.

Chapter 44

MEDITATION FOR THE HALL OF RECONNECTION

The Hall of Reconnection is Romanesque in design, with many golden columns and a foyer that leads to two huge brass doors. You enter this temple by yourself. Your guide and angels are certainly not abandoning you here; they are giving you some privacy so that you will not feel self-conscious when you meet the loved one with whom you want to reconnect. This does not mean that you will be unable to spend time with your guide, but rather that those meetings are more suited to other areas or other buildings. This is a time when even on the Other Side you can go in privately to have a personal talk with someone you love so dearly.

If you want to reconnect with a lost love, you can do so. But as strange as it sounds, you may also want to see someone with whom you had difficulty in life—not a dark entity, but someone whom you just could not seem to come to grips with. It could also be a father who passed before you were born or a person whom you would simply like to have a long discussion with. You go over to one of the marble benches that has a silvery, fluffy down cushion on it, and you can sit there for as long as you wish and talk.

There are so many kindred souls with whom you can have a private conversation, and you have a wonderful mind-merge.

So many times in life there is not enough time to talk, but here you have all the time in the world. You can sit and speak to a sibling you never knew or a mother you felt abandoned you . . . you can resolve things to get an understanding.

You also can call on a great mind if you want, since we all know each other on the Other Side. But again it is so marvelous to connect with individuals who are specifically attached to you or maybe someone from a past life. This is also an excellent place for you to get close to people who have passed over. You can reconnect because you enjoyed them so much that you want to have another conversation with them.

You can even have your guide come in, but as I said earlier, this hall is really meant as a place to link up with lost or past loved ones, and you can be with your guide in any area on the Other Side. The Hall of Reconnection is truly meant as a place to see your loved ones, to go over things, to embrace them, and to get out all the thoughts you wish you could have shared but never got the chance to. How many times have we said that?

So use this meditation as often as you like, for it will fulfill you and make you feel as if you have never left anything unsaid or undone. Then come back, all the way back to yourself, knowing that everything is perfectly all right and you can visit your passed-over loved ones whenever you need to: one . . . two . . . three.

Chapter 45

MEDITATION FOR THE HALL OF HEALING

The magnificent Hall of Healing is probably the most stunning of all the Romanesque temples. It has large pillars in front and a huge glass dome on the roof that projects a beautiful and healing green light to the entire interior of the hall. There is also an ebonized statue of the Mother God on a pedestal in the center of the building, standing in all Her beauty, with a sword in Her hand, which is not for violent purposes but to symbolize that She can cut through negativity and illness. Always remember that Her sword makes a cross.

There are many golden-glass cubicles shaped like pyramids inside this temple, and you are encouraged by attendants to go into one of them for treatment. This by no means is ever to take the place of seeing your physician or psychologist when you need help—the Hall of Healing is just another tool that our Creators provide to assist you.

You go into one of these cubicles and lie on top of a marble bed with a very fluffy mattress on it. The attendants come over and run their hands over you, and some have rods with orbs at the top. They can take away depression and any illness, even a chronic one.

All of a sudden you are aware of dancing lights that move throughout your body, trading pain for warmth and pleasure.

Blue is at the top of your head for peace of mind, green brings serenity throughout your entire being . . . so too will these dancing lights open up all the chakras in your body and then protect them. Use visualization to help augment the therapeutic effect of this pyramid and the ever-present lights—especially the green healing one. Ask that your ailment be cured.

Leave yourself in the cubicle for as long as you wish, feeling totally uplifted and pain free, for there really will not be pain in your body. Ask Azna to use Her sword to cut through any remaining negativity, and bask in the love that She, the angels, and your guide bring you. Go to this temple as many times as you wish and stay for as long as you want.

Come back, all the way back to yourself now, feeling ultimately renewed, refreshed, and invigorated: one . . . two . . . three.

Chapter 46

MEDITATION FOR THE TEMPLE OF AZNA
(THE MOTHER GOD)

The Temple of Azna is probably the most ornate of all the temples, as it has golden columns with gold-leaf lotus patterns at the top, and its impressive dome glows with a silvery light. Inside are more wonders, including chiffonlike veils of every color, and a light breeze seems to blow them back and forth constantly. There are gorgeous stained-glass windows that go from the floor to the ceiling that appear to move and change with the illustrations depicted, ranging from continents to animals.

The floor is made of a silvery type of marble that gives off a continuous luminescent glow, and there is a beautiful golden cauldron that is at least 50 feet across taking up more than one-third of the floor's space. This cauldron is so important because it is where all the petitions to our Mother that have been sent by those of us in life end up.

Standing behind the cauldron is a statue of Her, which is at least 60 feet high. She is depicted in a lovely, flowing, and filmy floor-length dress with Her ever-present sword in Her right hand. The statue changes colors periodically from ebony into gold, purple, green, and then to white. And if you ask to see and talk to Her, the stone will immediately begin to change colors, and the eyes will look right at you. It is at this point that She will come down off of Her pedestal and be fully animated, in all Her love and glory.

She has a hands-on approach and will give you all the information and love that you have never, ever experienced from any other source; after all, She is a mother. You can ask Her anything, and you will get an instantaneous reply.

Now She says, "Everything in creation has always existed, for creation has no beginning and no end. There is no such thing as time because everything has, is, and will happen all at once. As God I am the past, present, and future and you are a part of Me and therefore past, present, and future as well. You are like a molecule of My body . . . I experience what you have experienced, what you are experiencing now, and what you will experience; and all that experience is already residing within Me. So everything that is always was, and because of that, I am part of you and you are part of Me, and that love goes on for eternity."

If you say this to yourself in a meditative state, I can tell you from experience that there is something about the phrase "I am part of you and you are part of Me," and the knowledge that you are part of the molecular structure of this Divine Mother, which will magnify your soul. You will expand your consciousness beyond anything you can ever imagine.

After you have seen our blessed Azna, you can go to Her beautiful gardens to sit and contemplate the blessings She has given you, for you cannot see Her and be with Her without getting a blessing. Stay here as long as you want, and then come back, all the way back to yourself, feeling absolutely marvelous, better than you have ever felt before: one . . . two . . . three.

♦ ♦ ♦

Chapter 47

MEDITATION FOR THE TEMPLE OF THE FATHER GOD

The Temple of the Father God is by far the most interesting hall because of how it has impacted the architecture of our world. This gigantic cathedral is made of the most brilliant pink-gold spires that rise hundreds of feet in the air, and there are even golden doors. It does not have a cross on top, and the windows depict scenes and vignettes of human life instead of saints or holy images. It is like pictorial stained glass.

It is not ornate inside this temple, except for the golden pillars and a type of altar that seems to be surrounded by a golden mist. There are three steps leading up to the altar, which is made of golden marble and has huge gilded candlesticks on top of it, in which the candles are always lit. Now remember, you do not grovel or kneel, but you know you are in the presence of the Creator. God may show Himself as an old man, but He usually appears as a beautiful young male with coiffed, curly hair that almost looks like a "Caesar cut." But Father God chooses not to hold a visage for very long.

Nevertheless, you feel His emanation, and oh, you feel the euphoria of our Father in His magnificence and ethereal beauty. He is not as activated or as verbal as our Mother—it is more a communion of the soul with Him. But to be in His presence is truly overwhelming, for you are in the presence of your very own DNA.

How could you ever think that you are not worthy enough to be with our Maker? During the brief moment that you see Him, His beautiful eyes pierce your soul with love. There is never, ever any criticism or judgment. In fact, you feel the weight of all your lives coming off. It is almost as if He is whispering to you, "You have done well, good and faithful person that you are—the person I have created, the person I have made. You have been on a long journey, and maybe you have been prodigal at some time, but you are My beloved. I love you, and that will never change. I have unconditional love for you."

You are not exactly floored by these words but are rather just so filled with gratitude. There is no euphoria that compares to this. This is a sublime love that no soul mate or friendship, be it animal or human, could ever compare to. You are now in the sight of the great and glorious God the Father, our Father Who art in heaven, our Father Who art with you now, our Father Who loves you no matter what, our Father Who forgives you no matter what.

There is no shame, no penance or penitence, and no feeling of guilt. All of that is washed away. You feel His laughter and His joy; and even if you cannot see Him except for a few moments, you know His presence is there. A silver mist envelops you almost like He has His arms around you.

Most people will not want to do this next part of the meditation, but feel free to do so if you want to peek at the seventh level. So right behind the golden altar in the Temple of the Father God is a type of curtain, and if you part it, you can see where the uncreated mass ends up. This is where people who want to merge into the Godhead and lose their identity go. When you do part the curtain, you see all their faces for a moment, and they are beautiful.

Now this is also where the dark entities will eventually go, into the uncreated mass at the end of this schematic. Even though they divided themselves from Him thanks to their own egos, in His magnificent justice and love, He will not destroy them. These entities are here for a purpose because this planet is a hellhole, and without them we might not learn. Yet at the end of this schematic, they will no longer be useful, so God in His infinite mercy will reabsorb them.

At least we are not harangued by them on the Other Side, thank God—literally, thank God. The Divine Prima Mobile is the reason we are all here, and is what holds us and keeps us in place. He rules the universe and everything within it. . . .

No matter what type of earthly parents you had, you now understand the Father's love. This is God, and He adores you! To be able to be in the presence of your beloved Maker, there is nothing better than that. And He is not the God of jealousy or animosity, of discrimination or of judgment—He is just pure, accepting love, never asking more of you than you can bear, even though you may have disagreed at times. But now you are so proud of yourself that you went through those hardships, that you survived hell and can proudly stand in front of Him.

What you thought were your foibles have gone away, thanks to being in the presence of a loving Father. Whether you want to call him God, Jehovah, Yahweh, Allah, El, or Om, it doesn't matter. He is the I Am, the alpha and the omega, the beginning and the end of everything, the circle, and the now. No soul is lost. No rock drops that He does not know about. There is not an eye that blinks that He does not know about. He sees and cares about every move you make, and He is always, <u>always</u> with you.

Basking in the Divine Father's loving presence, you realize that you are now truly advancing to the pinnacle of your spirituality. He can even implant a sliver of light within you so that wherever you step, you can plant His light of love throughout the world. You have been imbued with this light, from the top of your head to the tip of your toes, which you can use to get rid of darkness. You can walk around negative people and rid them of that negativity or at least get them away from you. You are a pillar of light.

So as you turn reluctantly on your heel and go out the door, you know that you have been in the presence of Divinity—

and I mean true Divinity, just as with Mother God—and the infusion of love and the feeling of being precious and unique is with you forever. Now you know your purpose. You have come to the end of your spiritual journey this time, yet you can always go back and begin another part of it. It never ends . . . not here, not anywhere. You are continually getting closer to your soul's perfection.

You walk out of this glorious temple and come back to yourself now, feeling that you are full of the Divine and that you almost sparkle with the silver and gold love, and you will never forget it. You will never be without it.

Now come back, all the way back to yourself, feeling absolutely marvelous, better than you have ever felt before: one . . . two . . . three.

AFTERWORD

I genuinely had no prior in-depth knowledge of most of the sites mentioned in these pages until quite recently. Oh sure, I'd been told about a few of them, but I didn't give much thought to inquiring further and took the information as it came. I'm sure that I was so entranced by what I'd learned from helping people through hypnosis and hearing about their astral-travel and near-death experiences that I got caught up in not seeing the forest for the trees.

It really never occurred to me that there were so many beautiful and functional temples on the Other Side and that we learn so much from them—or have so much fun in them. It was just wonderful to have Francine give me the details about each of these new halls. The great thing about Gnosticism is that it keeps growing with knowledge, and I believe that because we're nearing the end of times for our planet, more and more information will come in. It makes my heart sing, and I feel so blessed and humble to be one of the vessels to make that happen.

No matter what religion or belief system you have, you'll come Home and be free because the truth will open you up, and you'll realize that it's not only your authentic habitat, but your true reality. You'll understand that your life on Earth is transient, a school to experience negativity and be tested by it to advance your soul.

By using the meditations I've presented here (or your own), you'll be able to visit these wondrous temples on the Other Side for yourself and experience their truly *miraculous* effects . . . and I don't use that word lightly. People who have visited them seem to enjoy greater health and well-being and accelerated spirituality.

I truly hope this book and its exercises bring you as much joy as I have had in bringing this information to you.

God love you. I do.
Sylvia

ABOUT THE AUTHOR

Sylvia Browne is the #1 *New York Times* best-selling author and world-famous psychic medium who appears regularly on *The Montel Williams Show* and *Larry King Live,* as well as making countless other media and public appearances. With her down-to-earth personality and great sense of humor, Sylvia thrills audiences on her lecture tours and still has time to write numerous immensely popular books. She has a master's degree in English literature and plans to write as long as she can hold a pen.

Sylvia is the president of the Sylvia Browne Corporation; and is the founder of her church, the Society of Novus Spiritus, located in Campbell, California. Please contact her at: **www.sylvia.org**, or call **(408) 379-7070** for further information about her work.

NOTES

NOTES

NOTES

NOTES

NOTES

NOTES

NOTES

NOTES

NOTES

NOTES

We hope you enjoyed this Hay House book.
If you would like to receive a free catalogue featuring additional
Hay House books and products, or if you would like information
about the Hay Foundation, please contact:

Hay House UK Ltd
292B Kensal Rd • London W10 5BE
Tel: (44) 20 8962 1230; Fax: (44) 20 8962 1239
www.hayhouse.co.uk

***

Published and distributed in the United States of America by:
Hay House, Inc. • PO Box 5100 • Carlsbad, CA 92018-5100
Tel.: (1) 760 431 7695 or (1) 800 654 5126;
Fax: (1) 760 431 6948 or (1) 800 650 5115
www.hayhouse.com

Published and distributed in Australia by:
Hay House Australia Ltd • 18/36 Ralph St • Alexandria NSW 2015
Tel.: (61) 2 9669 4299; Fax: (61) 2 9669 4144
www.hayhouse.com.au

Published and distributed in the Republic of South Africa by:
Hay House SA (Pty) Ltd • PO Box 990 • Witkoppen 2068
Tel./Fax: (27) 11 467 8904 • www.hayhouse.co.za

Published and distributed in India by:
Hay House Publishers India • Muskaan Complex • Plot No.3
B-2 • Vasant Kunj • New Delhi – 110 070.
Tel.: (91) 11 41761620; Fax: (91) 11 41761630.
www.hayhouse.co.in

Distributed in Canada by:
Raincoast • 9050 Shaughnessy St • Vancouver, BC V6P 6E5
Tel.: (1) 604 323 7100; Fax: (1) 604 323 2600

***

Sign up via the Hay House UK website to receive the Hay House
online newsletter and stay informed about what's going on with
your favourite authors. You'll receive bimonthly announcements
about discounts and offers, special events, product highlights,
free excerpts, giveaways, and more!
www.hayhouse.co.uk